KNITTING TRADITIONS

KNIT 25 SCANDINAVIAN, ICELANDIC AND FAIR ISLE ACCESSORIES

SUSAN ANDERSON-FREED

KRAUSE PUBLICATIONS
CINCINNATI, OHIO

CONTENTS

INTRODUCTION

I fell in love with Fair Isle knitting in 1992 when I discovered Alice Starmore's *Book of Fair Isle Knitting*. We were spending a year at the Institute for Advanced Studies in Princeton, New Jersey, which was an easy drive to The Tomato Factory Yarn Company in Lambertville. Skeins of wonderfully colored Shetland jumper-weight yarn lined the shelves of this delightful store. I bought enough yarn for several sweaters on our initial excursion and thus began my foray into Fair Isle knitting. Along with detailed instructions, Starmore's book furnished a new vocabulary that included steeks and peerie patterns. I fondly remember ordering skeins of natural, nondyed Shetland wool whose color names still captivate me: Gaulmogot, Katmollet, Yuglet, Mooskit, Moorit and Shaela.

After ten years I began experimenting with glove and mitten design. I started by using my adaptations of Fair Isle designs on the glove or mitten body. I gradually added peerie patterns to the fingers and thumbs. A trip to Iceland in 2009 introduced me to the uniquely beautiful nineteenth-century Icelandic weaving and embroidery patterns. I adapted several patterns first to glove and mitten designs and later to the other projects featured in this book.

The patterns, with the exception of the Jenny and Susan designs, are each named after one of my chemotherapy nurses. Each pattern's name also reflects the image that a traditional pattern evoked when I began redesigning it. For example, a stepped cross reminded me of Navajo weaving, and I began to transform the base design into a pattern that resembled a Navajo rug (see the *Susan's Storm* patterns on pages 20, 44 and 120). In another instance, I chose a heart design and enlarged it to include a flower on the inside (see the *Shirley's Snow Heart* patterns on pages 80 and 100). I changed each traditional design in this manner. In most cases, the original base design is barely recognizable.

I hope you enjoy knitting these projects as much as I enjoyed creating them!

Susan

STRANDED KNITTING TECHNIQUES

Since stranded or two-color knitting is in the round, the right side of the piece is always in front of the knitter. This results in fewer pattern mistakes and much greater knitting speeds. I generally prefer to hold my yarns on either side of my middle finger as shown below, left.

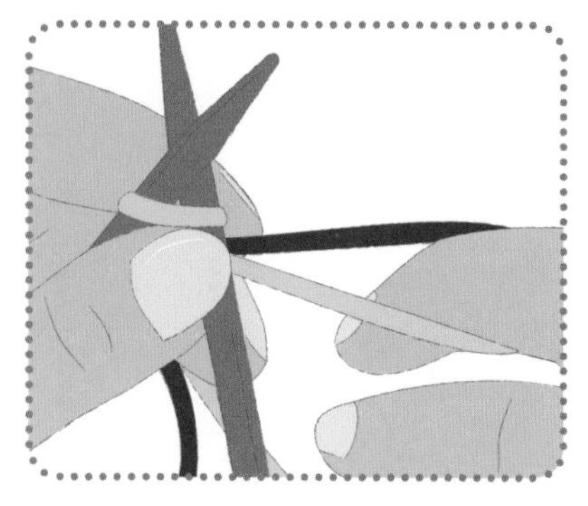

Yarn Placement

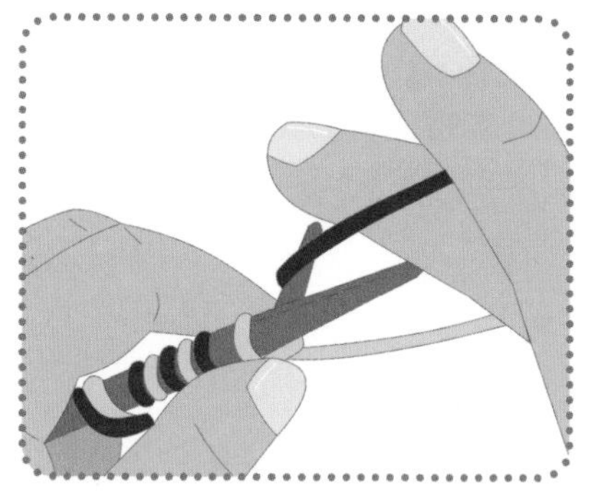

Knit with MC

To knit with the main color (MC) yarn, use the outside edge of your middle finger to lift the yarn into place.

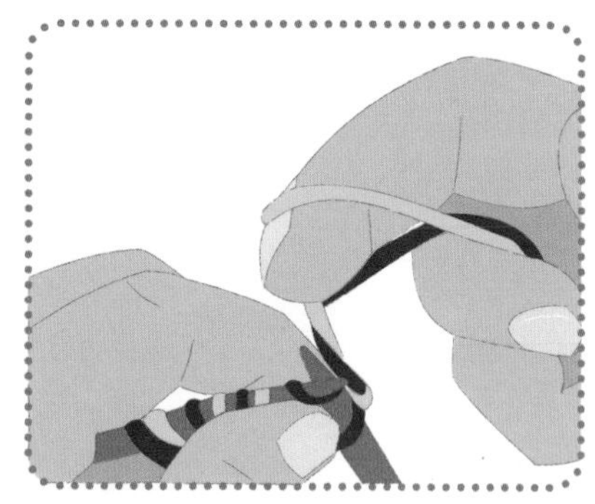

Knit with CC

To knit with the contrasting color (CC) yarn, use the inside of your middle finger to lift the yarn into place.

TIPS AND TRICKS

If you're new to Fair Isle knitting, here are a few pointers I'd like to share.

Tangled Yarn

Inevitably the yarns will tangle. To untangle them, simply place one strand of yarn in each hand and let your knitting hang down. Your garment will start to spin, with each revolution removing one twist. It's quite fun to watch.

Reading Patterns

Because knitting is in the round, read all patterns from right to left. Since I don't like to count the stitches knit in each color, if a pattern contains more than four consecutive stitches in the same color, I indicate that in the pattern. For example, in the simple chart at right, the diamonds in Rounds 3 and 5 contain five consecutive red stitches. Rounds 1 through 7 each contain at least one set of five consecutive white stitches. Be careful to watch for consecutive stitches wrapping from the end to the beginning of the next pattern repeat.

Yarn Carries

When a pattern indicates that more than three to four stitches are knit in a single color, always carry the yarn along the back of the work. To do this, simply bring the yarn that isn't being knit over the working yarn.

I also carry the yarns when I change colors. To do this, break off the old yarns and switch to the new yarns. Knit the pattern in the new colors. On the next round, tie the old and new yarns into a knot. As you knit each stitch, bring the yarn tails over the working yarn. Do this for ten to twelve stitches. Wait a few rounds before trimming the loose ends. Not only does this technique secure the loose ends, but it saves you time later.

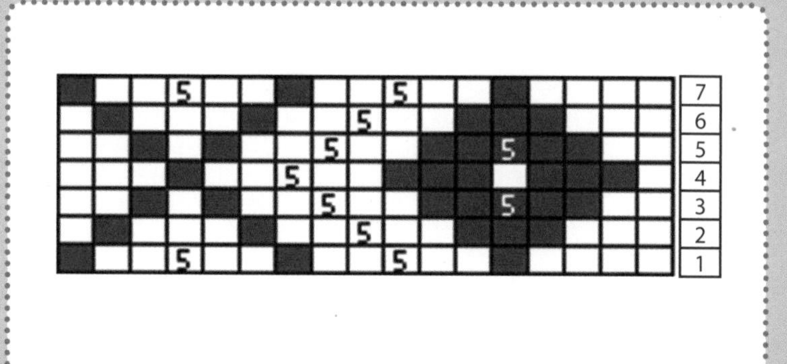

MATERIALS AND TOOLS

YARNS

I've knit the patterns in this book using two different weights of yarn.

The leg warmers use worsted-weight yarn while the remaining projects use fingering or sock-weight yarn. The leg warmers use a 50/50 alpaca/wool blend for greater sturdiness.

For the remaining projects, any fingering or sock-weight yarn works well. Since the gauge is small (typically eight and a half or nine stitches per inch [2.5cm]), differences in skein yardage produce slight, if any, difference in the finished size of a project.

Although I suggest specific yarns for each garment, I've knit many of the projects using other yarns. All of the yarns worked well, and there are several fingering-weight yarns that I am eager to try.

For a complete list of yarns I used for this book, consult the *Resources* section on page 140.

The glove palms, sock and knee-high leg and foot borders and sole, as well as the leg warmer borders, use small repeating (peerie) patterns. The legends indicate that you should use the dark or light yarn because these colors change as the glove, sock, knee-high or leg warmer main pattern colors change.

For the dark yarn, use the darker color. For the light yarn, use the lighter color. If there is only one dark color or light color, that color is indicated in the legend.

For example, *Sabrina's Ojo de Dios Knee-Highs* (see page 114) use only Black as the dark yarn, and *Lyndi's Feathered Star Socks* (see page 94) use only Natural as the light yarn.

NEEDLES

The pattern directions for the gloves and mittens suggest one set each of 6" (15cm) and 8" (20.5cm) double-pointed needles in the size required for the indicated gauge. I do not use a separate set of needles in a smaller gauge for the ribbing because all of the garments use corrugated ribbing, which tends to be inherently tighter.

I also prefer 10" (25.5cm) or 12" (30.5cm) double-pointed needles over circular needles for the hats, tams and leg warmers because it causes less wear and tear on my thumbs.

If you choose to make the garments using alpaca yarn, I highly recommend bamboo needles because the yarn is less likely to slip off the needles.

As a final note, the needle sizes are based on my gauge. I knit very loosely. In contrast, my daughter knits much more tightly. When she test knit several tams, she increased the needle size significantly.

ADDITIONAL EQUIPMENT

In addition to yarn and needles, you'll find the following tools helpful when knitting the garments.

Row Counter

This gadget comes in handy when knitting the corrugated knitting or salt-and-pepper rounds.

Stitch Markers

Since it's far easier to correct a mistake when found early, I use stitch markers to separate the pattern repeats for the hats and tams.

Safety Pins

I use large quilting safety pins to secure the live stitches of the fingers and thumbs when making gloves and mittens.

Tam Frame or Plate

The tams require stretching over a tam frame or a plate. Since tam frames are hard to come by, a 9" (23cm) plastic dinner plate works fairly well. You can usually pick these up in sets of four at a discount store.

CHAPTER ONE

HATS AND TAMS

STOCKING HATS

I always keep an arsenal of hats to battle the cold Illinois winters. Included in my list of favorites is the simple stocking or watch hat. Even a gusty wind cannot dislodge these head-hugging beauties. The stocking hats included in this section use a ribbed selvedge to give them greater head-hugging abilities and provide extra warmth for the ears.

CUSTOMIZING THE HATS

For a shorter hat, reduce the number of rounds of ribbing. For a longer hat, add rounds to the ribbing or knit additional rounds in the peerie pattern before beginning the crown decreases.

For a wider hat, add a stitch to each side of the vertical peerie band. Each pair of stitches adds about an inch (2.5cm) to the circumference. Keep in mind that any changes to the circumference require changes in the crown decreases.

SIZE

One size fits most women

MEASUREMENTS

Circumference: 19" (48cm)

Length: 9" (23cm)

NEEDLES

One 10" (25.5cm) set of US 2 (2.75mm) double-pointed needles or a 24" (61cm) circular needle

One 8" (20.5cm) set of US 2 (2.75mm) double-pointed needles (optional)

If necessary, change needle size to obtain correct gauge.

NOTIONS

Stitch markers

Tapestry needle

GAUGE

4" (10cm) = 36 sts and 36 rnds in salt-and-pepper pattern

WHAT IS A PEERIE?

A peerie pattern is a small repeating pattern typically used as a "filler" or border in Fair Isle knitting.

HAT

Note: MC and CC are indicated in your chosen design.

With MC, cast on 144 sts onto 3 needles—48 sts on each needle.

SELVEDGE

Work 17 rnds of corrugated ribbing as follows: K2 MC, p2 CC.

Hem Rnd: Purl 1 rnd in MC.

Work 18 rnds of corrugated ribbing using the Corrugated Ribbing Pattern specific to your chosen design.

Knit 1 rnd in MC while increasing 8 sts on each needle—168 sts.

BODY

Follow the Hat Chart indicated by your chosen design through Rnd 37.

Dec Rnds 38–51: *Knit the 7-stitch vertical band following the chart, sl 1, k1, psso, knit to the last 2 sts of the main pattern, k2tog. Repeat from * 3 more times.

Dec Rnds 52–53 : *Sl 1, k1, psso, knit to the last 2 sts of the vertical band, k2tog, sl 1, k1, psso, knit to the last 2 sts of the main pattern, k2tog. Repeat from * 3 more times.

Dec Rnd 54: *Sl 1, k2tog, psso. Repeat from * around—8 sts.

After the last decrease, k2tog around with MC. Draw the yarn tightly through the remaining 4 sts.

FINISHING

Turn the Hat inside out. Fold the hem at the Hem Rnd and tack into place on the inside of the Hat using a tapestry needle.

Weave in all ends and block.

HEATHER'S BROKEN STAR HAT

YARN

5 skeins of fingering weight yarn (approx 231yds [211m] per 1.76oz [50g]) in 5 different colors: Fairy Tale (MC), Cotton Candy (CC), Blossom Heather, Blush and Cream

The project shown was made using Knit Picks Palette (100% Peruvian Highland wool, 1.76oz/50g, 231yds/211m) in Fairy Tale, Cotton Candy, Blossom Heather, Blush and Cream.

CORRUGATED RIBBING PATTERN

Rnds 1–3: K2 Fairy Tale, p2 Cotton Candy.

Rnds 4–5: K2 Fairy Tale, p2 Blossom Heather.

Rnds 6–7: K2 Fairy Tale, p2 Blush.

Rnds 8–11: K2 Fairy Tale, p2 Cream.

Rnds 12–13: K2 Fairy Tale, p2 Blush.

Rnds 14–15: K2 Fairy Tale, p2 Blossom Heather.

Rnds 16–18: K2 Fairy Tale, p2 Cotton Candy.

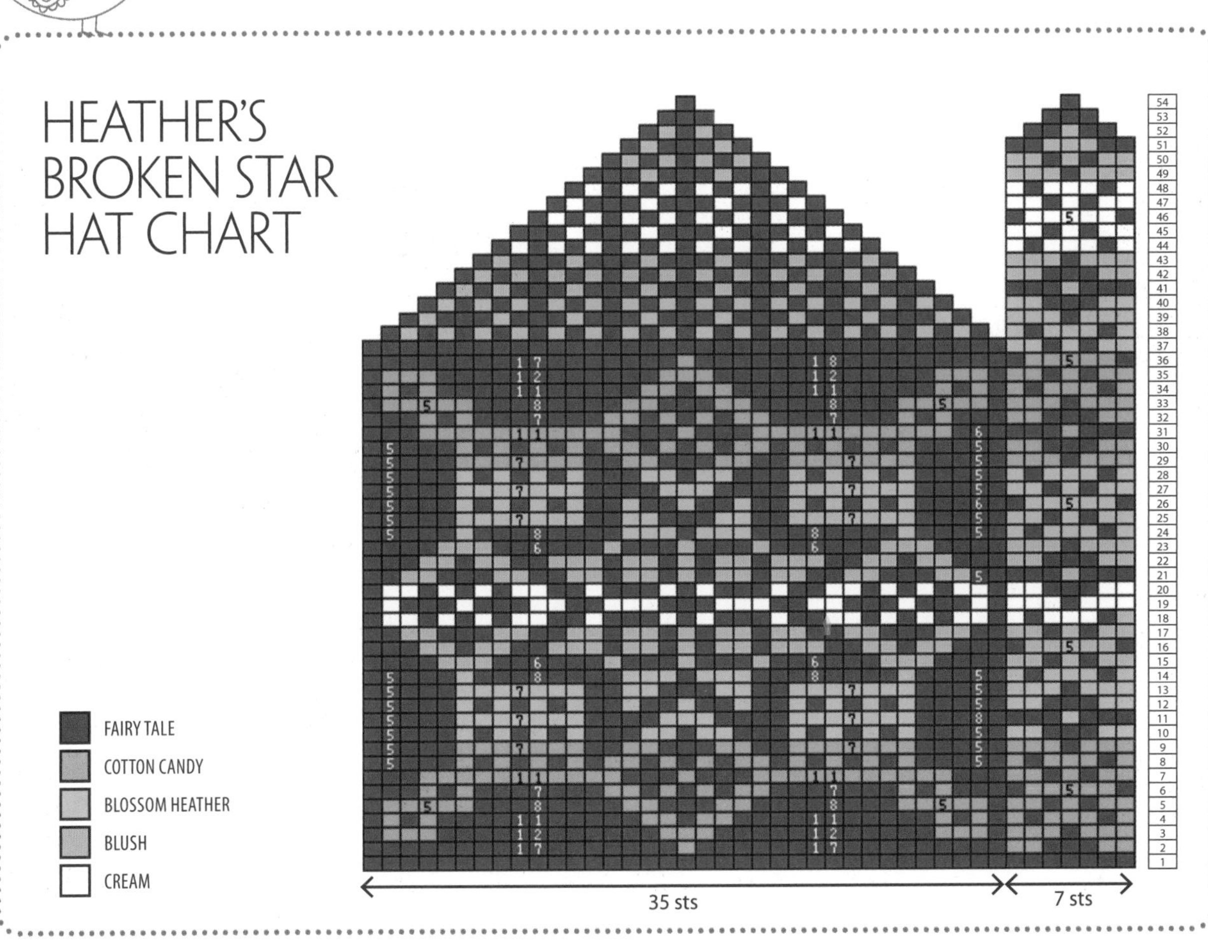

HEATHER'S BROKEN STAR HAT

ALTERNATE COLORWAY

YARN

5 skeins of fingering weight yarn (approx 231yds [211m] per 1.76oz [50g]) in 5 different colors: Clematis (MC), Cherish (CC), Light Blue, Pale Aqua and Vanilla

This alternate colorway uses Madelinetosh Tosh Sock (100% merino wool, 4oz/114g, 395yds/361m) in Clematis, Rowan Yarn Cashsoft 4 Ply (wool/microfiber/cashmere, 1.76oz/50g, 197yds/180m) in Cherish, and Sublime Baby Cashmere Merino Silk 4 Ply (merino/silk/cashmere, 1.76oz/50g, 186yds/170m) in Light Blue, Pale Aqua and Vanilla.

CORRUGATED RIBBING PATTERN

Rnds 1–3: K2 Clematis, p2 Cherish.

Rnds 4–5: K2 Clematis, p2 Light Blue.

Rnds 6–7: K2 Clematis, p2 Pale Aqua.

Rnds 8–11: K2 Clematis, p2 Vanilla.

Rnds 12–13: K2 Clematis, p2 Pale Aqua.

Rnds 14–15: K2 Clematis, p2 Light Blue.

Rnds 16–18: K2 Clematis, p2 Cherish.

HEATHER'S BROKEN STAR HAT CHART

ALTERNATE COLORWAY

- CLEMATIS
- CHERISH
- LIGHT BLUE
- PALE AQUA
- VANILLA

35 sts

7 sts

JEANNE'S SUNBURST HAT

YARN

6 skeins of fingering weight yarn (approx 231yds [211m] per 1.76oz [50g]) in 6 different colors: Regal (MC), Periwinkle (CC), Baby Blue, Lilac, Papaya and Soft Peach

The project shown was made using Knit Picks Palette (100% Peruvian Highland wool, 1.76oz/50g, 231yds/211m) in Regal and Plymouth Baby Alpaca DK (100% alpaca, 1.76oz/50g, 125yds/114m) in Periwinkle, Baby Blue, Lilac, Papaya and Soft Peach.

CORRUGATED RIBBING PATTERN

Rnds 1–3: K2 Regal, p2 Periwinkle.

Rnds 4–5: K2 Regal, p2 Baby Blue.

Rnds 6–7: K2 Regal, p2 Soft Peach.

Rnds 8–11: K2 Regal, p2 Papaya.

Rnds 12–13: K2 Regal, p2 Soft Peach.

Rnds 14–15: K2 Regal, p2 Baby Blue.

Rnds 16–18: K2 Regal, p2 Periwinkle.

JEANNE'S SUNBURST HAT CHART

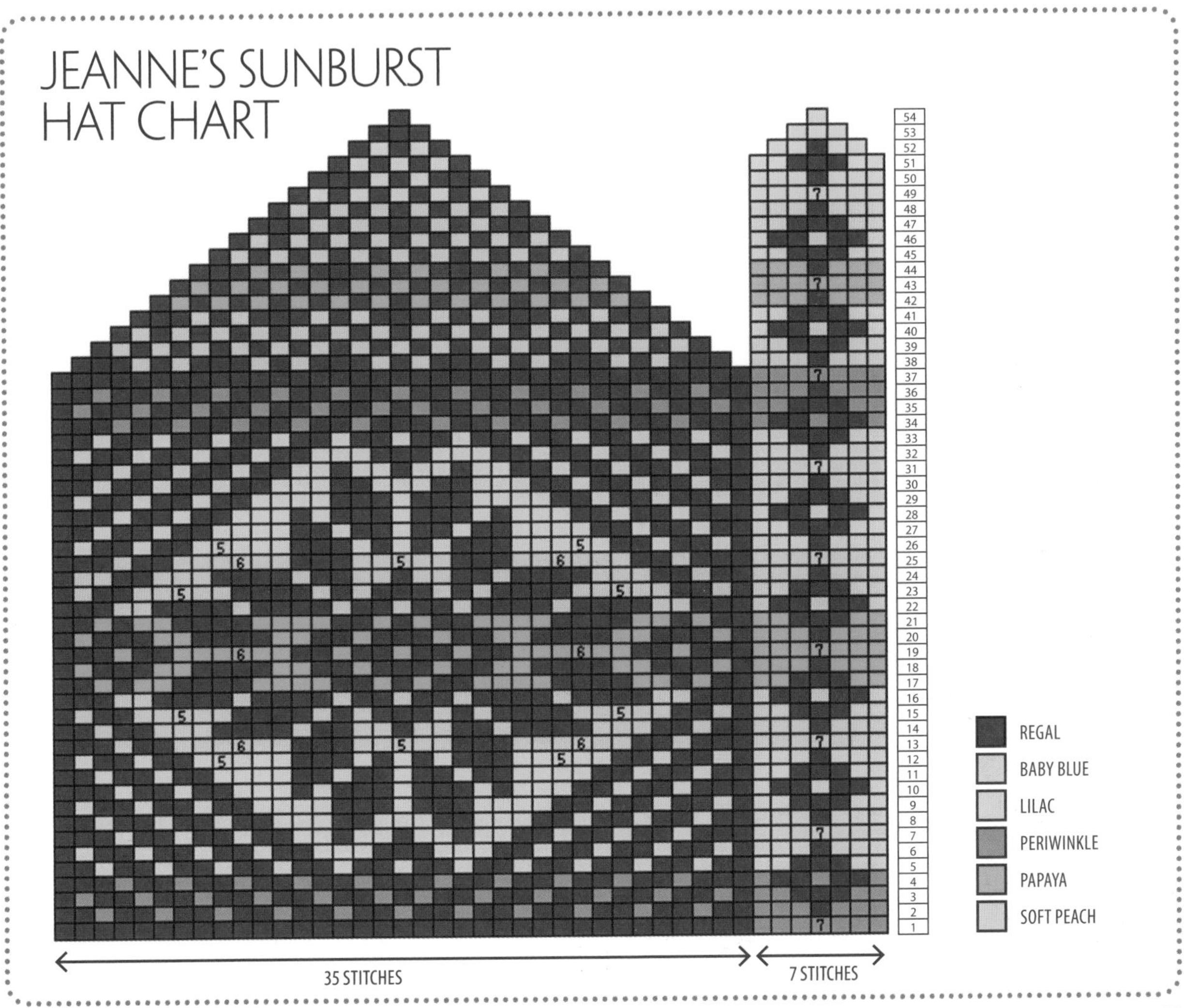

JEANNE'S SUNBURST HAT

ALTERNATE COLORWAY

YARN

6 skeins of fingering weight yarn (approx 231yds [211m] per 1.76oz [50g]) in 6 different colors: Black Magic (MC), Clematis (CC), Purple Mountain Majesty, Dahlia, Tart and Peach

This alternate colorway was made using The Alpaca Yarn Company Glimmer (alpaca/polyester, 1.76oz/50g, 183yds/167m) in Black Magic and Purple Mountain Majesty, Madelinetosh Tosh Merino Light (100% merino wool, 3.5oz/100g, 420yds/384m) in Dahlia, Madelinetosh Tosh Sock (100% merino wool, 4oz/114g, 395yds/361m) in Tart and Clematis, and Sublime Baby Cashmere Merino Silk 4 Ply (merino/silk/cashmere, 1.76oz/50g, 186yds/170m) in Peach.

CORRUGATED RIBBING PATTERN

Rnds 1–3: K2 Black Magic, p2 Peach.

Rnds 4–5: K2 Clematis, p2 Peach.

Rnds 6–7: K2 Dahlia, p2 Peach.

Rnds 8–11: K2 Tart, p2 Peach.

Rnds 12–13: K2 Dahlia, p2 Peach.

Rnds 14–15: K2 Clematis, p2 Peach.

Rnds 16–18: K2 Black Magic, p2 Peach.

JEANNE'S SUNBURST HAT CHART

ALTERNATE COLORWAY

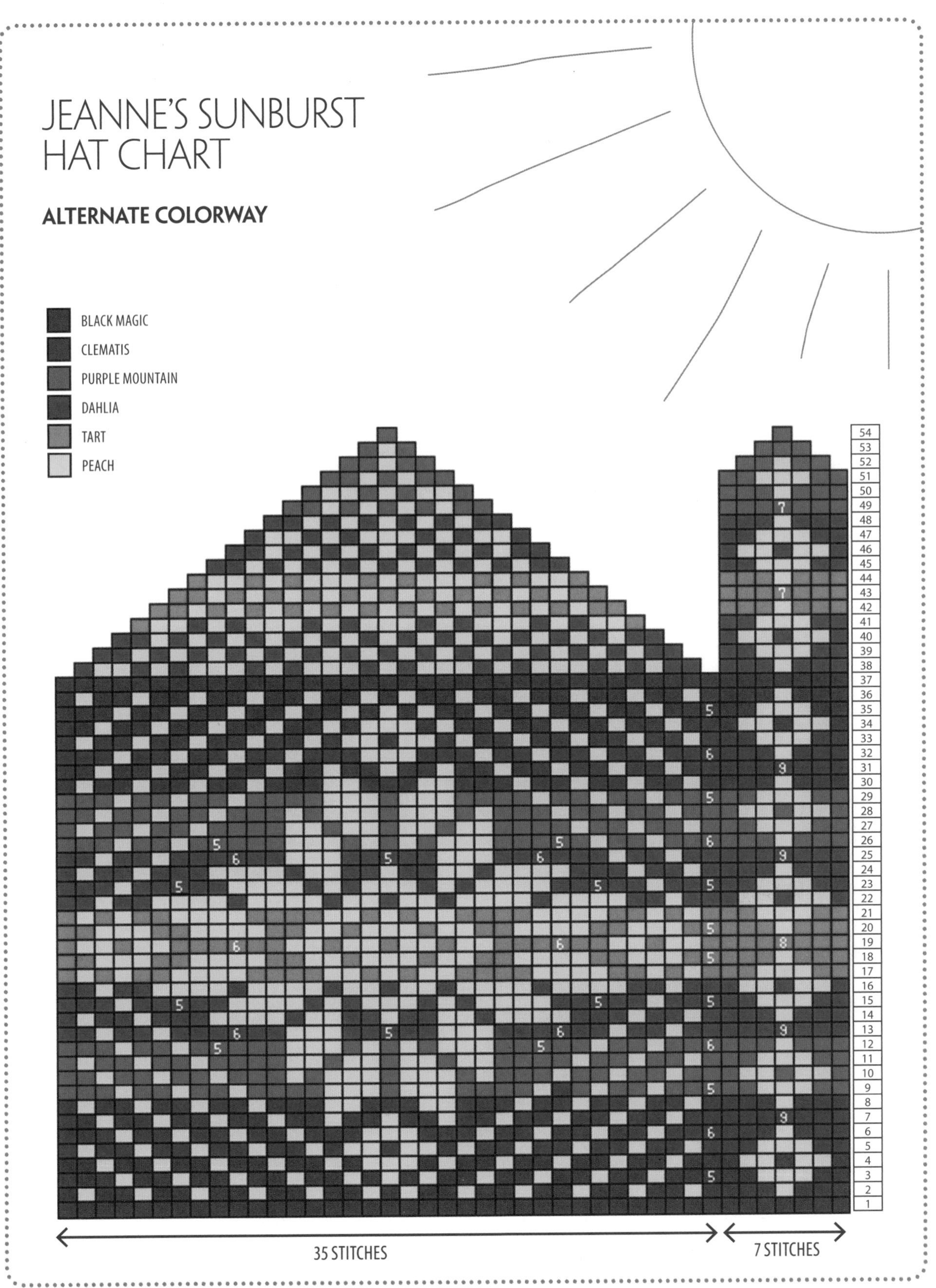

SUSAN'S STORM HAT

YARN

6 skeins of fingering weight yarn (approx 231yds [211m] per 1.76oz [50g]) in 6 different colors: Timber (MC), Oyster Heather (CC), Blush, Mai Tai Heather, Mint Kiss and Icicle

The project shown was made using Knit Picks Gloss Fingering (merino/silk, 1.76oz/50g, 220yds/201m) in Timber, Knit Picks Palette (100% Peruvian Highland wool, 1.76oz/50g, 231yds/211m) in Oyster Heather, Mai Tai Heather and Blush, and The Alpaca Yarn Company Glimmer (alpaca/polyester, 1.76oz/50g, 183yds/167m) in Mint Kiss and Icicle.

CORRUGATED RIBBING PATTERN

Rnds 1–2: K2 Timber, p2 Oyster Heather.

Rnds 3–4: K2 Timber, p2 Blush.

Rnds 5–6: K2 Timber, p2 Mai Tai Heather.

Rnds 7–8: K2 Timber, p2 Mint Kiss.

Rnds 9–10: K2 Timber, p2 Icicle.

Rnds 11–12: K2 Timber, p2 Mint Kiss.

Rnds 13–14: K2 Timber, p2 Mai Tai Heather.

Rnds 15–16: K2 Timber, p2 Blush.

Rnds 17–18: K2 Timber, p2 Oyster Heather.

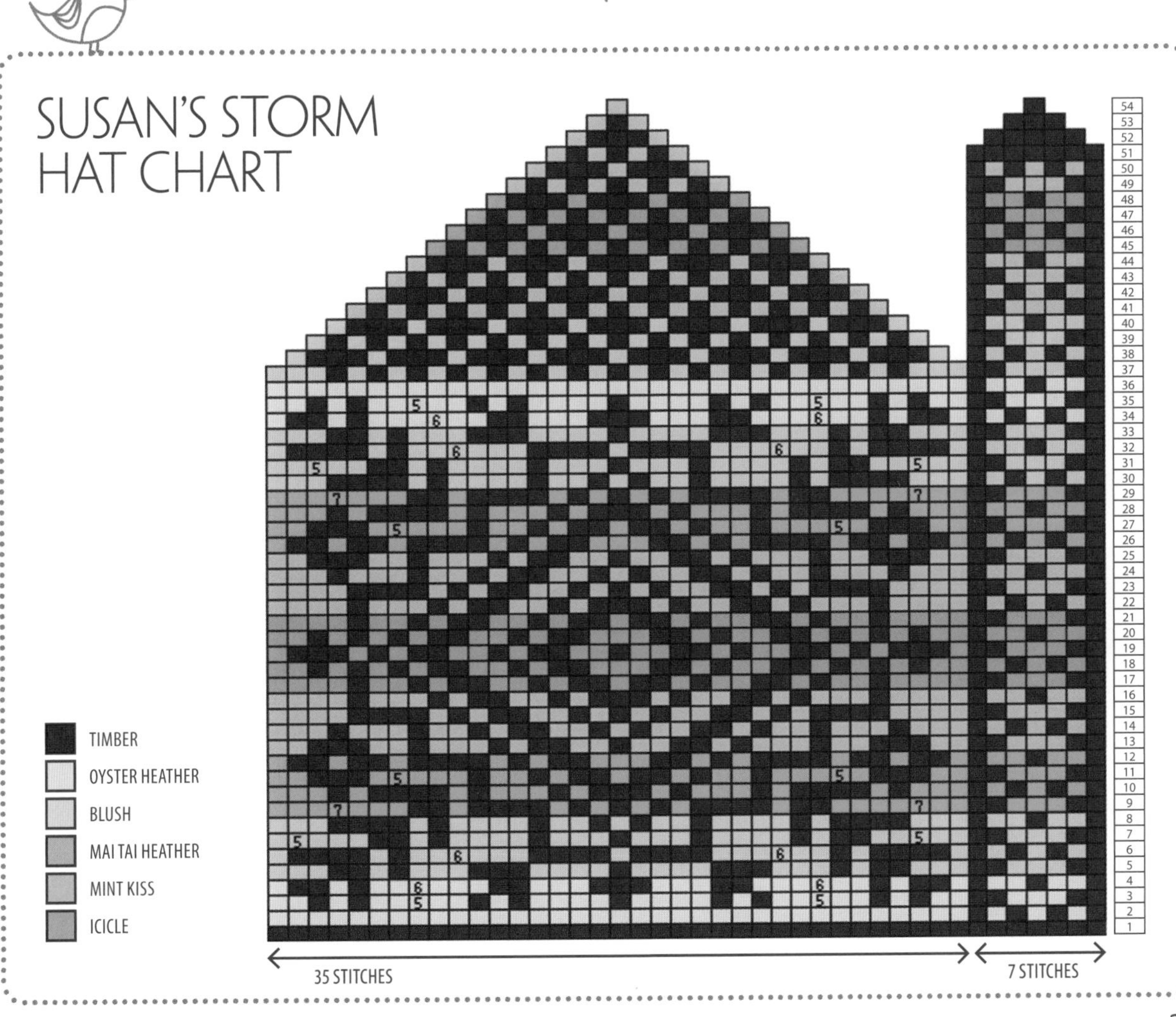

TAMS

I discovered Mary Rowe's *Knitted Tams* in 1992 while spending a year at the Institute for Advanced Studies in Princeton, where my husband was a visiting scholar. This delightful book provided a wonderful diversion from the computer science text I was writing. I knit more than twenty tams that year, all with seven points, as illustrated by Ms. Rowe's book. However, nestled in this book was a suggestion that tam crowns need not have only seven points. Applying my computer science skills, I designed tam crowns with points ranging from five to eighteen. Of course, this only fueled my tam-making obsession. I designed tams with stars, medallions and leafs in the crowns.

I was satisfied until I discovered Kenneth Libbrecht's wonderful books of snowflake photography in 2008. Could I design tam crowns that resembled snowflakes? The answer appears in this section, where I've included *Jenny's Snowflake Tam* (see page 24) and *Laurie's Twelve-Point Petal Tam*, which is really a double snowflake (see page 28).

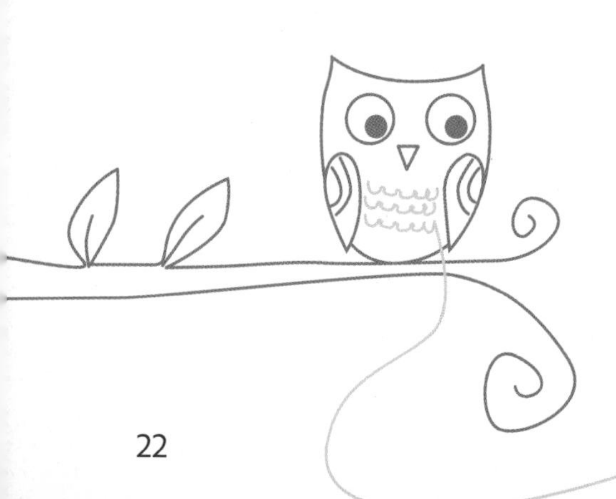

SIZE

One size fits most women

MEASUREMENTS

Circumference: 19" (48cm)

NEEDLES

One 10" (25.5cm) set of US 2 (2.75mm) double-pointed needles or a 24" (61cm) circular needle

One 8" (20.5cm) set of US 2 (2.75mm) double-pointed needles (optional)

If necessary, change needle size to obtain correct gauge.

NOTIONS

Stitch markers

Tapestry needle

GAUGE

4" (10cm) = 36 sts and 36 rnds in salt-and-pepper pattern

ANATOMY OF A TAM

All tams begin with corrugated ribbing. Although this type of ribbing lacks the elasticity of k2, p2 ribbing, its vivid color changes produce a beautiful finished look. The technique used to produce corrugated ribbing is simple: Knit two stitches in one color and purl two stitches in a second color. Upon completion of the ribbing, knit two repeats of the tam brim chart. One repeat forms the lower brim, which you'll see when the tam wearer faces you. The second repeat forms the upper or top brim, which you'll see when the tam wearer has her back to you.

FINISHING YOUR TAM

To block your tam into a wearable circular shape, stretch it over a plate or tam frame. Begin by soaking the tam in a wool wash such as Eucalan. Remove most of the moisture from the tam by wrapping it in a towel or sending it through the spin cycle on your washer. Stretch the tam over a 9" (23cm) plate or a tam frame and let it dry.

JENNY'S SNOWFLAKE TAM

YARN

6 skeins of fingering weight yarn (approx 231yds [211m] per 1.76oz [50g]) in 6 different colors: Jay, Eggplant, Regal, Mist, Pennyroyal and Oyster Heather

The project shown was made using Knit Picks Palette (100% Peruvian Highland wool, 1.76oz/50g, 231yds/211m) in Jay, Eggplant, Regal, Mist, Pennyroyal and Oyster Heather.

CORRUGATED RIBBING PATTERN

Rnds 1–3: K2 Jay, p2 Mist.

Rnds 4–5: K2 Eggplant, p2 Pennyroyal.

Rnds 6–8: K2 Regal, p2 Oyster Heather.

Rnds 9–10: K2 Eggplant, p2 Pennyroyal.

Rnds 11–13: K2 Jay, p2 Mist.

TAM

With Jay, cast on 144 sts onto 3 needles—48 sts on each needle.
Follow the Corrugated Ribbing Pattern for 13 rnds.
Knit 1 rnd with Oyster Heather while increasing 10 sts each on Needles 1 and 3 and 12 sts on Needle 2—176 sts.

BRIM

* Work Rnds 1–17 of the Tam Brim and Top Chart. Knit 1 rnd with Oyster Heather. Repeat from * once.
Knit 1 rnd with Jay while increasing 4 sts evenly around—180 sts.

TAM WHEEL

Note: This pattern uses a 30-stitch repeat which produces a 6-point wheel.
All Decreases Except Those on Rnds 7, 25 and 27: Sl 2 as if to knit, k1, p2sso.
Rnds 7 and 25 Decreases: Sl 1, k2tog, psso.
Rnd 27 Decreases: K2tog around with Jay.
After the last decrease, 6 sts remain. Draw these through tightly with the yarn.

FINISHING

Weave in all ends and block.

JENNY'S SNOWFLAKE TAM CHART

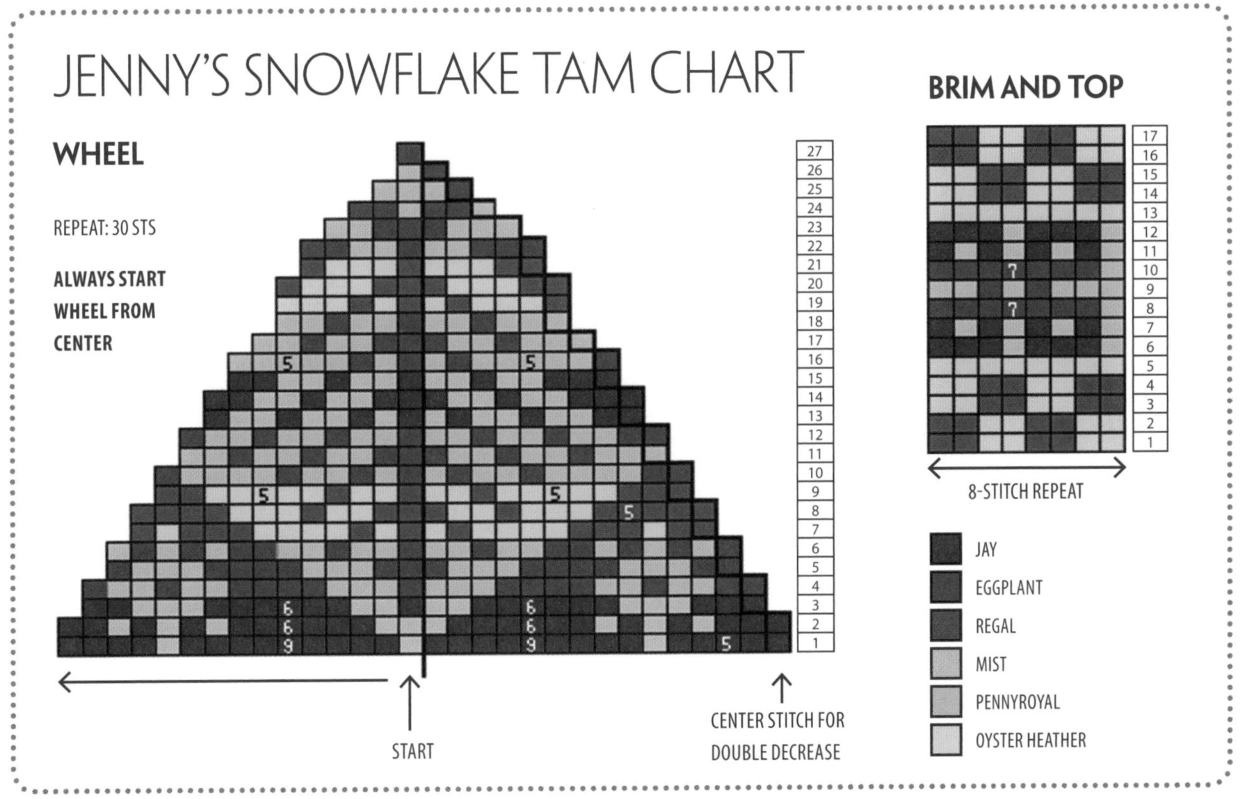

KATEY'S OUTLINED STAR TAM

YARN

7 skeins of fingering weight yarn (approx 231yds [211m] per 1.76oz [50g]) in 7 different colors: Bark, Fig, Vandyke Brown, Byzantine, Camel, Boston Beige and White House

The project shown was made using Cascade Yarns Heritage 150 Solids (merino/nylon, 5.3oz/150g, 492yds/450m) in Bark, Cascade Yarns Heritage Silk (merino/silk, 3.5oz/100g, 437yds/400m) in Camel and Vandyke Brown, The Alpaca Yarn Company Classic Lite (100% alpaca, 1.76oz/50g, 182yds/166m) in Boston Beige and White House, and Madelinetosh Tosh Merino Light (100% merino wool, 3.5oz/100g, 420yds/384m) in Byzantine and Fig.

CORRUGATED RIBBING PATTERN

Rnds 1–3: K2 Bark, p2 Camel.

Rnds 4–5: K2 Fig, p2 Camel.

Rnds 6–8: K2 Byzantine, p2 White House.

Rnds 9–10: K2 Fig, p2 Camel.

Rnds 11–13: K2 Bark, p2 Camel.

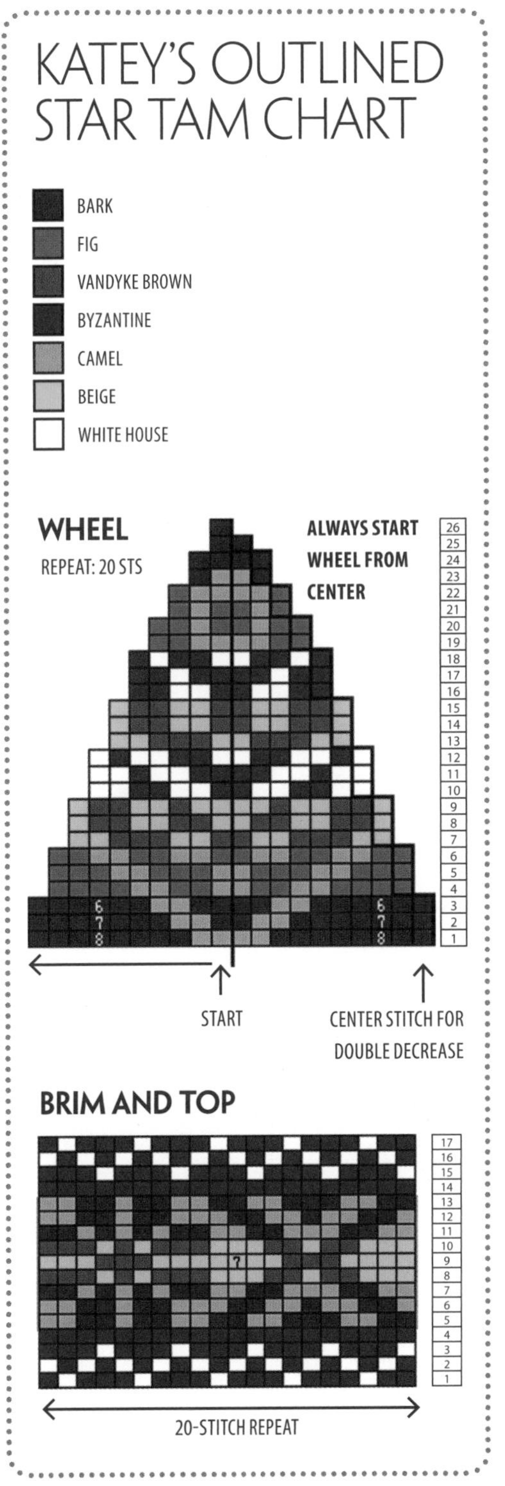

TAM

With Bark, cast on 144 sts onto 3 needles—48 sts on each needle.
Follow the Corrugated Ribbing Pattern for 13 rnds.
Knit 1 rnd with Byzantine while increasing 12 sts on each needle—180 sts.

BRIM

Work Rnds 1–17 of the Tam Brim and Top Chart. Knit 2 rnds with Byzantine.
Work Rnds 1–17 of the Tam Brim and Top Chart. Knit 1 rnd with Byzantine.
Knit 1 rnd with Bark.

TAM WHEEL

Note: This pattern uses a 20-stitch repeat, which produces a 9-point wheel.
All Decreases Except Those on Rnd 26: Sl 2 as if to knit, k1, p2sso.
Rnd 26 Decreases: K2tog with Bark.

After the last decrease, 9 sts remain. Draw these through tightly with the yarn.

FINISHING

Weave in all ends and block.

LAURIE'S TWELVE-POINT PETAL TAM

YARN

6 skeins of fingering weight yarn (approx 231yds [211m] per 1.76oz [50g]) in 6 different colors: Loganberry, Amethyst, Quartz, Mosaic, Cream and Elite

The project shown was made using Rowan Yarn Cashsoft 4 Ply (wool/microfiber/cashmere, 1.76oz/50g, 197yds/180m) in Loganberry, Amethyst, Quartz, Mosaic, Cream and Elite.

CORRUGATED RIBBING PATTERN

Rnds 1–3: K2 Loganberry, p2 Elite.

Rnds 4–5: K2 Amethyst, p2 Elite.

Rnds 6–8: K2 Quartz, p2 Cream.

Rnds 9–10: K2 Amethyst, p2 Elite.

Rnds 11–13: K2 Loganberry, p2 Elite.

TAM

With Loganberry, cast on 144 sts onto 3 needles—48 sts on each needle.
Follow the Corrugated Ribbing Pattern for 13 rnds.
Knit 1 rnd with Loganberry while increasing 10 sts on Needles 1 and 3 and 12 sts on Needle 2—176 sts.

BRIM

*Work Rnds 1-17 of the Tam Brim and Top Chart. Knit 1 rnd with Loganberry. Repeat from * once. Knit 1 rnd with Mosaic while increasing 4 sts evenly—180 sts.

TAM WHEEL

Note: This pattern uses a 15-stitch repeat, which produces a 12-point wheel.
Rnd 15 Decreases: K3tog.
Rnds 19, 22 and 24 Decreases: K2tog, s1, k1, psso. (This preserves the double line.)
All Other Decreases Including Those on Rnd 26: Sl 2 as if to knit, k1, p2sso.
Note: On Rnd 26, move the first stitch on Needle 1 to Needle 3 prior to beginning decreases.
After the last decrease, 12 sts remain. Draw these through tightly with the yarn.

FINISHING

Weave in all ends and block.

LAURIE'S TWELVE-POINT PETAL TAM CHART:

BRIM AND TOP

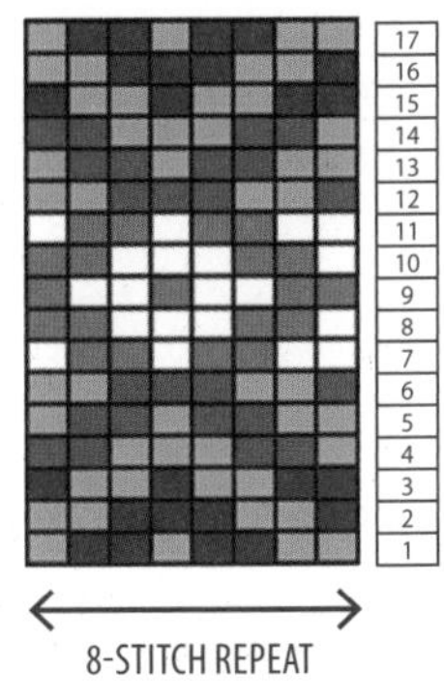

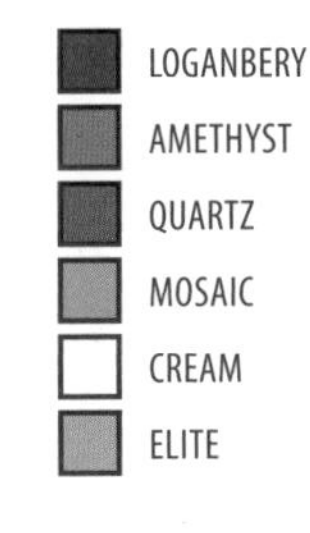

WHEEL

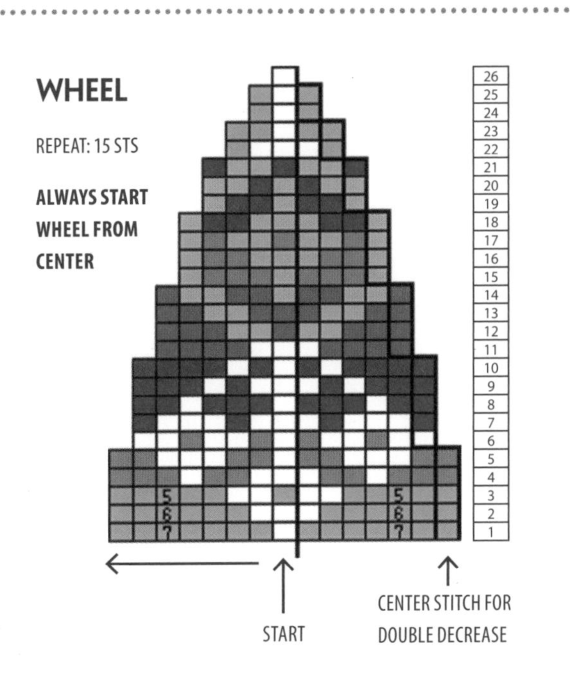

LYNDI'S NINE-POINT ALLOVER TAM

YARN

5 skeins of fingering weight yarn (approx 231yds [211m] per 1.76oz [50g]) in 5 different colors: Turquoise, Nebula, Forestry, Jade and Natural

The project shown was made using Cascade Yarns Heritage Silk (merino/silk, 3.5oz/100g, 437yds/400m) in Turquoise, Madelinetosh Tosh Merino Light (100% merino wool, 3.5oz/100g, 420yds/384m) in Nebula, Forestry and Jade, and Knit Picks Bare Gloss Merino Wool/Silk Fingering Weight (merino/silk, 3.5oz/100g, 440yds/402m) in Natural.

CORRUGATED RIBBING PATTERN

Rnds 1–3: K2 Turquoise, p2 Natural.

Rnds 4–5: K2 Forestry, p2 Natural.

Rnds 6–8: K2 Jade, p2 Natural.

Rnds 9–10: K2 Forestry, p2 Natural.

Rnds 11–13: K2 Turquoise, p2 Natural.

TAM

With Turquoise, cast on 144 sts onto 3 needles—48 sts on each needle.

Follow the Corrugated Ribbing Pattern for 13 rnds.

BODY

Knit 1 rnd with Turquoise while increasing 12 sts on each needle—180 sts.

Work Rnds 1-62 of Lyndi's Nine-Point Allover Tam Chart (see page 32).

All Decreases Except Those on Rnds 40, 43 and 62: Sl 2 as if to knit, k1, p2sso.

Rnd 40 and 43 Decreases: Sl 2 through the back loops, k1, p2sso.

Rnd 62 Decreases: K2tog through the back loops with Forestry.

After the last decrease, 9 sts remain. Draw these through tightly with the yarn.

FINISHING

Weave in all ends and block.

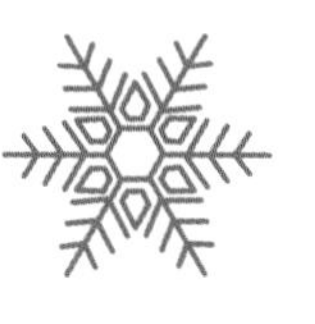

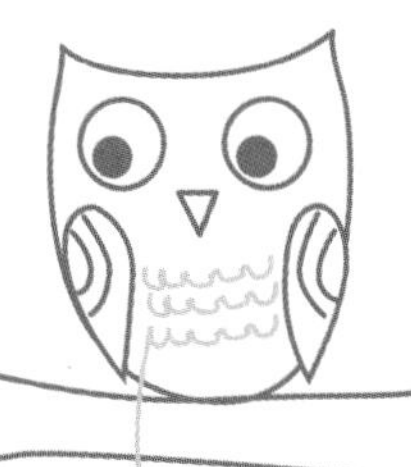

LYNDI'S NINE-POINT ALLOVER TAM

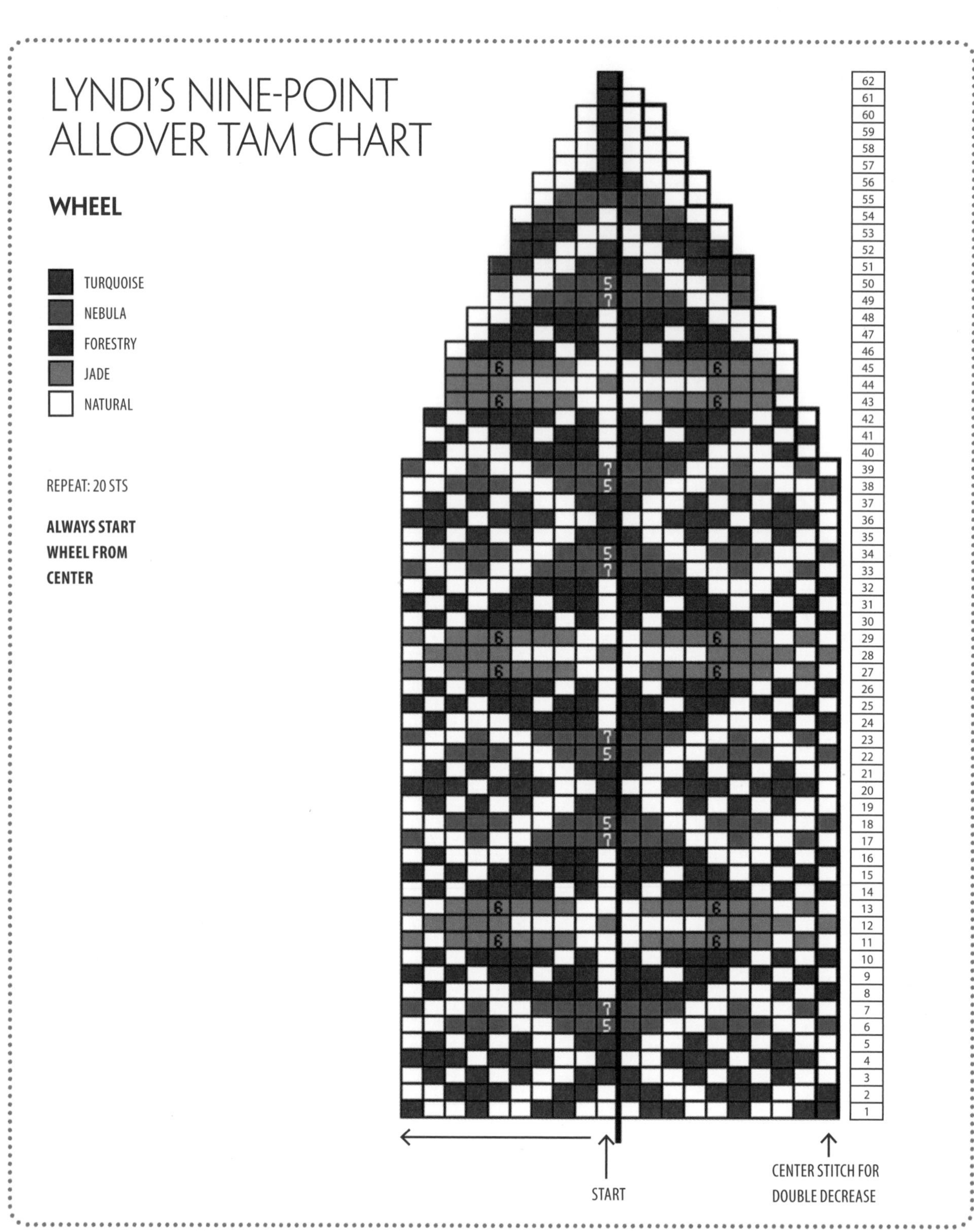

LYNDI'S NINE-POINT ALLOVER TAM CHART
WHEEL
TURQUOISE
NEBULA
FORESTRY
JADE
NATURAL
REPEAT: 20 STS
ALWAYS START WHEEL FROM CENTER
62
61
60
59
58
57
56
55
54
53
52
51
50
49
48
47
46
45
44
43
42
41
40
39
38
37
36
35
34
33
32
31
30
29
28
27
26
25
24
23
22
21
20
19
18
17
16
15
14
13
12
11
10
9
8
7
6
5
4
3
2
1
START
CENTER STITCH FOR DOUBLE DECREASE

CHAPTER TWO

MITTENS AND GLOVES

WOMEN'S MITTENS

ANATOMY OF A CROWN-TO-CUFF MITTEN

In the next section, you will find complete directions and graphs for the mitten designs in this book. Before starting, I want to familiarize you with the process used to knit *crown-to-cuff* mittens. All mittens begin with the thumb, which is knit first and placed on safety pins until needed. Unlike the usual way of knitting mittens, these thumbs have no apparent closure at the top, and you do not have the weight of the mitten body hanging down while working the thumb. The thumbs are interchangeable between the mittens; simply use the same colors specified for the mitten body.

The mitten body, as is true of the thumb, begins with a Turkish cast on—the cast on used for toe-up socks. A three-stitch border of alternating dark and light stitches separates the palm and back of the hand.

The crown is knit using increases that occur at each side of the border stitches on the mitten back and palm. After completing the crown increases, you will knit the mitten body. The palms use a small repeating pattern, which is interchangable with the other mitten designs. The back of the hand contains a larger star or snowflake pattern. The mitten graph shows both the palm and back of the hand as well as the thumb placement for the left and right mittens. The mitten directions indicate when to attach the thumb to the mitten. A 3-Needle Bind Off secures the palm and inside thumb stitches. Placement of the thumb depends on whether you are working the right or left mitten.

The mitten ends with twenty rounds of corrugated ribbing. Each mitten's instructions indicate the colors used for the corrugated ribbing.

For those who prefer cuff-to-crown mitten knitting, instructions are given at the end of the crown-to-cuff directions.

SIZE

One size fits most women

MEASUREMENTS

Length: 10¼" (26cm)

Circumference: 7" (18cm)

NEEDLES

One 6" (15cm) set of US 2 (2.75mm) double-pointed needles

One 8" (20.5cm) set of US 2 (2.75mm) double-pointed needles

If necessary, change needle size to obtain correct gauge.

NOTIONS

Safety pins

Stitch markers

Tapestry needle

GAUGE

4" (10cm) = 24 sts and 32 rnds in salt-and-pepper pattern

HINTS FOR KNITTING THE MITTEN CROWN AND THUMB

Be careful when knitting the cast-on stitches because knitting the stitches on the second needle can cause the stitches on the first needle to slip off the end of the needle.

Although the charts show four needles in action, excluding the needle doing the knitting, I typically only use three for ease in knitting. Feel free to divide the stitches as you see fit.

The initial three rounds are difficult because you have only a few stitches each on four needles. Once you make it past these rounds, the knitting becomes easier.

After Round 10 you may wish to weave the cast-on yarn tails to the inside of the crown or thumb. This not only gets the yarn out of your way, but it also saves you time later.

You will notice a gap on each side where the thumb joins the mitten body. To minimize a gap, slip the stitch before the gap. Pick up the left and right stitches one round before the gap. Knit these two stitches together. Pass the slipped stitch over the stitches and knit together as you would for sl 1, k2tog, psso. Do this for each side of the thumb. Any remaining gaps will be very small and you can use the tails remaining from the 3-Needle Bind Off to close this gap.

CROWN-TO-CUFF MITTENS

Note: All mittens use the same general technique. The mittens differ in the number and colors of yarns and occasionally in the total number of rounds. Each pattern contains a color list, ribbing chart, pattern charts and, if needed, special instructions.

THUMB

With the Turkish cast on (see page 138) and MC, cast on 6 sts onto the 6" (15cm) needles—3 sts on each needle. Knit across the sts on each needle.

Refer to the Thumb Chart for the desired pattern. Because the first rnd contains a single increase, it is easier to combine sts for Needles 1 and 2 onto the first needle and sts for Needles 3 and 4 on the pattern chart onto the second needle. This lessens the possibility of the sts slipping off the ends of the needle.

Thumb Rnd 1 (Increase Round):

1st Needle: Knit the 3 cast-on sts following the pattern for Needle 1. M1, following the pattern for Needle 2.

2nd Needle: Knit the 3 cast-on sts following the pattern for Needle 3. M1, following the pattern for Needle 4—8 sts.

On Rnd 2, divide the sts onto 4 needles.

Thumb Rnd 2 (Increase Rnd):

Needle 1: Knit the 3 sts following the pattern for Needle 1—1 st remains on the left needle.

Needle 2: With a new needle, Needle 2, IncR following the pattern for Needle 2. Knit the next stitch following the pattern for Needle 2. IncL following the pattern for Needle 2.

Needle 3: Knit the 3 sts following the pattern for Needle 3—1 st remains on the left needle.

Needle 4: IncR following the pattern for Needle 4. Knit the next stitch following the pattern for Needle 4. IncL following the pattern for Needle 4—12 sts.

Thumb Rnds 3–5 (Inc Rnds): Continue to follow the chart using the desired Thumb Chart, increasing 1 st at each end of Needle 2 and Needle 4—24 sts after Rnd 5.

Rnds 6–20: Follow the Thumb Chart for your pattern.

Rnd 21: Follow the Thumb Chart to the last stitch. Do not knit this stitch, but place it on Needle 1. Similarly, move the first stitch on Needle 4 to Needle 3—7 sts remain on Needle 4. Place these 7 inside-thumb sts on a safety pin. Divide the remaining sts between 2 safety pins.

BODY

Note: Each mitten is knit from the back of the hand to the palm side.

With the Turkish cast on and the 6" (15cm) needles, cast on 18 sts, using the color indicated by the Body Chart—9 sts on each needle.

Note: Most designs have a middle border stitch in a contrasting color.

Begin working the Body Chart as follows:

Rnd 1: Knit across the sts on Needle 1 (back-of-hand side). With Needle 2, M1 between the 2 cast-on needles following the chart. Knit approx half the sts from the palm side onto this needle. With a new needle (Needle 3), knit the remaining palm sts according to the chart. M1 between Needle 3 and Needle 1.

Rnds 2–12 (Inc Rnds):

Back-of-Hand Side Increases: Knit the first stitch, IncR. Follow the chart to the last stitch, incL. Knit the last stitch.

Palm Side Increases: Knit the first 2 sts, incR. Knit in the chart to the last 2 sts, incL. Knit the 2 remaining sts.

Note: Switch to the 8" (20.5cm) needles when the sts become cramped.

Rnd 13: Increase on the back-of-hand side only.

Rnds 14–44: Follow the chart for your chosen design.

Rnd 45 (Attach Thumb):

Right Mitten: Knit following the chart until you reach the highlighted right mitten Thumb sts. Use the 3-Needle Bind Off to join 7 inside-thumb sts with the 7 highlighted right mitten sts. Place the 17 Thumb sts onto the needle. Knit the Thumb sts using the Thumb Gusset Chart. Knit the remaining sts following the Body Chart.

Left Mitten: Knit in pattern until you reach the highlighted left mitten Thumb sts. Use the 3-Needle Bind Off to join the 7 inside-thumb sts with the highlighted left mitten palm sts. Place the 17 Thumb sts onto the needle. Knit the Thumb sts using the Thumb Gusset Chart. Knit the remaining sts following the Body Chart.

Rnds 46–61: Continue to follow the Body and Thumb Charts for your chosen design.

CUFF

Follow the final rnd(s) and Corrugated Ribbing Pattern for your chosen design.

FINISHING

Weave in all ends and block flat.

CUFF-TO-CROWN MITTENS

CUFF

Cast on 60 sts with MC. Knit 20 rnds of Corrugated Ribbing Pattern as specified by your chosen design.

BODY

Note: Each mitten is knit from the palm to the back of the hand. Turn all charts upside down to reorient them for cuff-up knitting.

On the first rnd of the pattern, increase the same number of sts as the ribbing decreases. At the same time, place Thumb gusset markers as follows:

Right Mitten: Knit border stitch, pm, knit the Thumb gusset sts as designated in the last Thumb Gusset Chart rnd (now the first rnd), pm. Start the palm side of the Body Chart at the first column to the left of the Thumb box; that is, draw a line down from the Thumb box's left edge (for the right mitten). Start the palm side of the Body Chart with the next st. Knit following the chart for the remainder of the rnd.

Left Mitten: Knit border stitch, knit sts in the palm side of the Body Chart until you reach the column containing the start of the left mitten Thumb box, pm, knit the Thumb gusset sts as designated in the last Thumb Gusset Chart rnd (now the first rnd), pm. Start the palm side of the Body Chart at the first column to the left of the Thumb box; that is, draw a line down from the Thumb box's left edge (for the left mitten). Knit following the chart for the remainder of the rnd.

Continue to follow the Body Chart and Thumb Gusset Chart until you reach the highlighted Thumb box on Rnd 45. Knit the sts following the last Thumb Gusset Chart rnd, then place the 17 Thumb sts on a holder. Continue to follow the charts for the rem of the rnd. On the next rnd, CO 7 sts using the palm side of the Body Chart in the space formerly occupied by the Thumb gusset sts.

Continue to follow the Body Chart until you reach Rnd 12 (which is now upside down). Decrease only on the back-of-hand side using the back-of-hand decreases. For the remaining rnds, except the last rnd, decrease on both the palm and back-of-hand sides as follows:

Palm Side Decreases: K1, sl 1, k1, psso, knit to last 3 palm sts, k2tog, k1.

Back-of-Hand Side Decreases: Sl 1, k1, psso, knit to last 2 sts, k2tog.

Last Decrease Rnd: Palm side only. These decreases remove the border sts. K2tog, knit to the last 2 sts, sl 1, k1, psso.

Kitchener stitch the remaining 18 sts.

THUMB

Remove the 17 Thumb sts from the holder and divide between 2 needles. The first and last sts will be placed with the Needle 4 sts on the Thumb chart. To do this, move the leftmost Thumb stitch to a new needle. Knit this stitch following the Thumb chart, then pick up and knit 7 sts following the pattern for Needle 4. (This is your rnd start.) Knit the next stitch onto Needle 4. Knit the remaining Thumb sts following the chart.

Knit following the Thumb Chart until Rnd 4.

Rnds 4, 3 and 2 Decreases: Sl 1, k1, psso, knit in pattern to the last 2 Needle 4 sts, k2tog, sl 1, k1, psso, knit in pattern to the last 5 sts, k2tog, knit remaining 3 sts in pattern.

Rnd 1 Decreases: *Sl 1, k2tog, psso, k3 in pattern. Repeat from * twice.

Last Dec Rnd: Move 1 rem Needle 3 stitch to Needle 1, k2tog, k2 in pattern, sl 1, k1, psso, knit to the end of the rnd.

FINISHING

Cut yarns. Draw remaining sts through with a loop and secure or Kitchener stitch them. Weave in all ends and block flat.

JEANNE'S SUNBURST MITTENS

YARN

6 skeins of fingering weight yarn (approx 231yds [211m] per 1.76oz [50g]) in 6 different colors: Regal (MC), Periwinkle, Baby Blue, Lilac, Papaya and Soft Peach

The project shown was made using Knit Picks Palette (100% Peruvian Highland wool, 1.76oz/50g, 231yds/211m) in Regal and Plymouth Baby Alpaca DK (100% alpaca, 1.76oz/50g, 125yds/114m) in Periwinkle, Baby Blue, Lilac, Papaya and Soft Peach.

MITTEN CONSTRUCTION

Follow the general directions through Rnd 61 using Jeanne's Sunburst Mittens Charts.

Rnd 62: Follow Jeanne's Sunburst Mitten Body Chart (see page 42).

Rnd 63: Knit this rnd with Regal while decreasing 6 sts evenly—60 sts.

CUFF

Work 20 rnds using the Corrugated Ribbing Pattern. Bind off in Regal.

CORRUGATED RIBBING PATTERN

Rnds 1–4: K2 Regal, p2 Periwinkle.

Rnds 5–6: K2 Regal, p2 Baby Blue.

Rnds 7–8: K2 Regal, p2 Soft Peach.

Rnds 9–12: K2 Regal, p2 Papaya.

Rnds 13–14: K2 Regal, p2 Soft Peach.

Rnds 15–16: K2 Regal, p2 Baby Blue.

Rnds 17–20: K2 Regal, p2 Periwinkle.

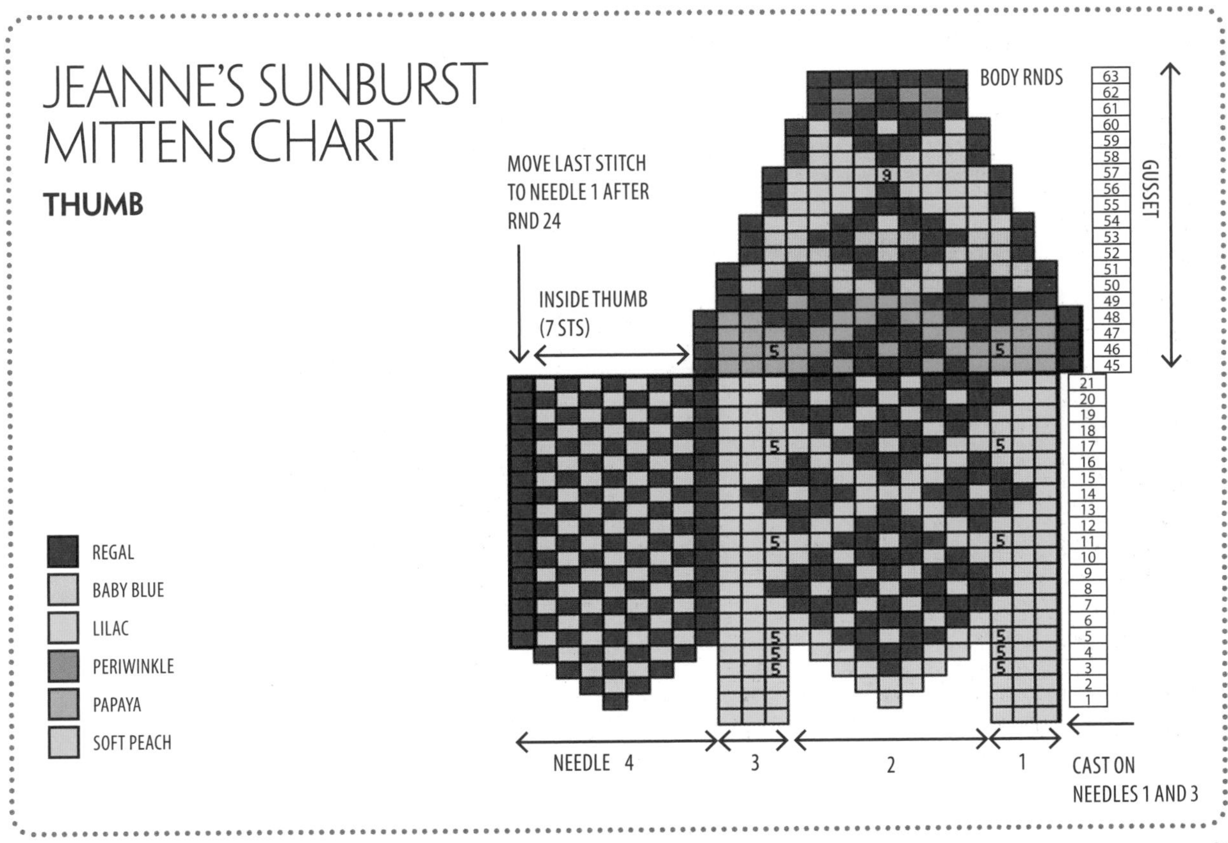

JEANNE'S SUNBURST MITTENS

JEANNE'S SUNBURST MITTENS CHART: **BODY**

CREATE THE LOOK
Jeanne's Sunburst Hat:
Page 16

SUSAN'S STORM MITTENS

YARN

6 skeins of fingering weight yarn (approx 231yds [211m] per 1.76oz [50g]) in 6 different colors: Timber (MC), Oyster Heather, Blush, Mai Tai Heather, Pennyroyal and Bluebell

The project shown was made using Knit Picks Gloss Fingering (merino/silk, 1.76oz/50g, 220yds/201m) in Timber and Knit Picks Palette (100% Peruvian Highland wool, 1.76oz/50g, 231yds/211m) in Oyster Heather, Blush, Mai Tai Heather, Pennyroyal and Bluebell.

MITTEN CONSTRUCTION

Follow the general directions through Rnd 61 using Susan's Storm Mittens Charts (see below and on page 46).

Rnds 62–63: Knit with Timber.

CUFF

Work 20 rnds using the Corrugated Ribbing Pattern. On the first rnd of ribbing, dec 6 sts evenly—60 sts. Bind off in Timber.

CORRUGATED RIBBING PATTERN

Rnds 1–2: K2 Timber, p2 Oyster Heather.

Rnds 3–4: K2 Timber, p2 Blush.

Rnds 5–6: K2 Timber, p2 Mai Tai Heather.

Rnds 7–8: K2 Timber, p2 Pennyroyal.

Rnds 9–12: K2 Timber, p2 Bluebell.

Rnds 13–14: K2 Timber, p2 Pennyroyal.

Rnds 15–16: K2 Timber, p2 Mai Tai Heather.

Rnds 17–18: K2 Timber, p2 Blush.

Rnds 19–20: K2 Timber, p2 Oyster Heather.

SUSAN'S STORM MITTENS CHART

THUMB

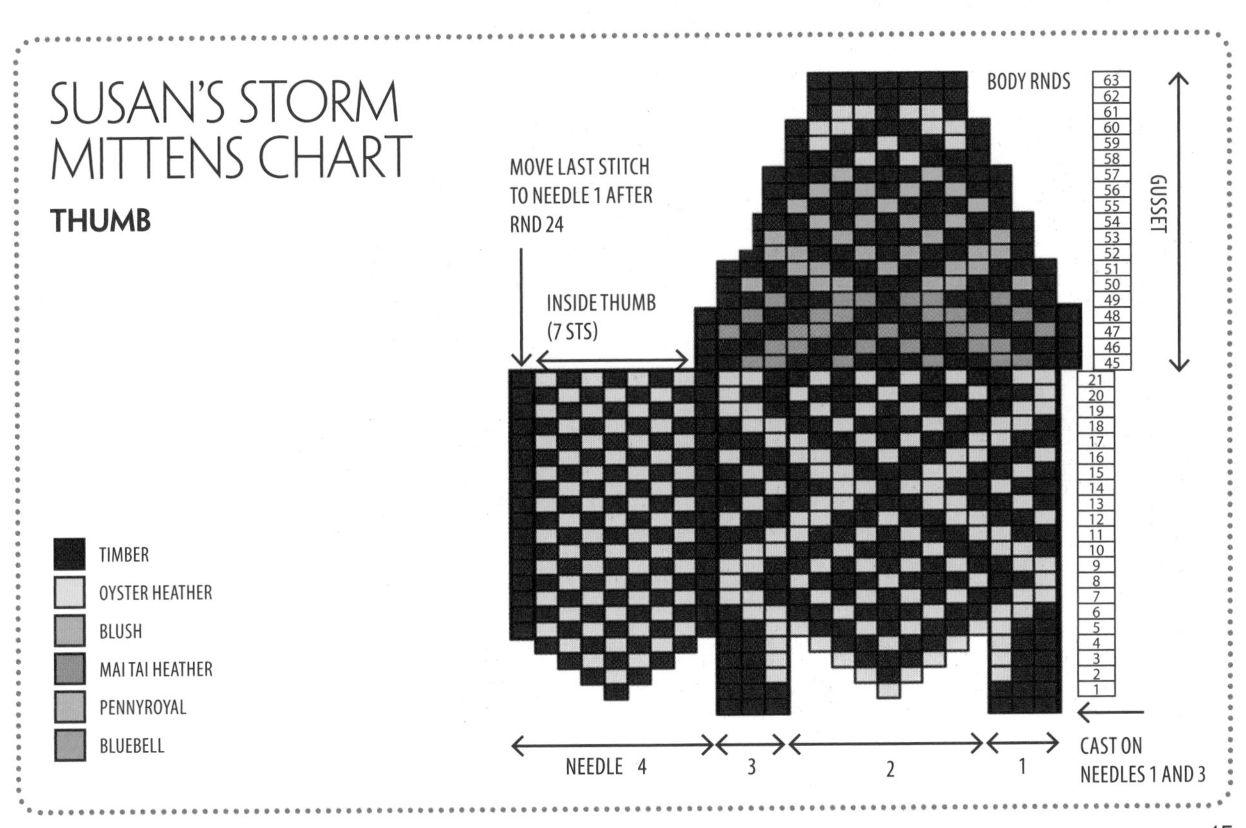

SUSAN'S STORM MITTENS

SUSAN'S STORM MITTENS CHART: BODY

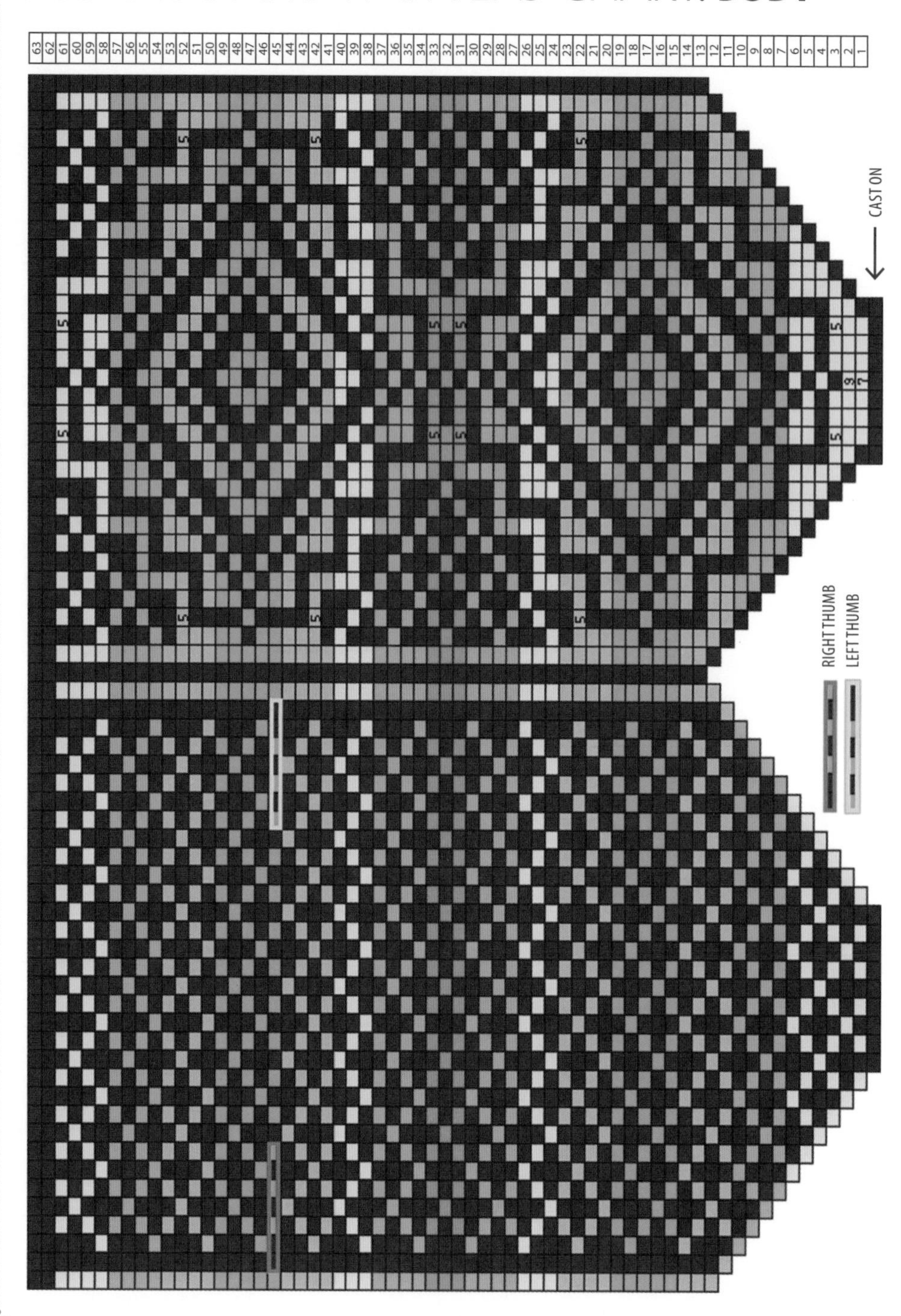

CREATE THE LOOK

Laurie's Twelve-Point Petal Tam: **Page 28**

LAURIE'S CHRYSANTHEMUM MITTENS

YARN

6 skeins of fingering weight yarn (approx 231yds [211m] per 1.76oz [50g]) in 6 different colors: Loganberry (MC), Amethyst, Quartz, Mosaic, Cream and Elite

The project shown was made using Rowan Yarn Cashsoft 4 Ply (wool/microfiber/cashmere, 1.76oz/50g, 197yds/180m) in Loganberry, Amethyst, Quartz, Mosaic, Cream and Elite.

MITTEN CONSTRUCTION

Follow the general directions through Rnd 61 using Laurie's Chrysanthemum Mittens Charts.

Rnd 62: Follow Laurie's Chrysanthemum Mittens Body Chart (see page 50).

Rnd 63: Knit with Elite while decreasing 6 sts evenly—60 sts.

CUFF

Work 20 rnds using the Corrugated Ribbing Pattern. Bind off in Loganberry.

CORRUGATED RIBBING PATTERN

Rnds 1–4: K2 Loganberry, p2 Elite.

Rnds 5–6: K2 Amethyst, p2 Elite.

Rnds 7–8: K2 Quartz, p2 Cream.

Rnds 9–12: K2 Mosaic, p2 Cream.

Rnds 13–14: K2 Quartz, p2 Cream.

Rnds 15–16: K2 Amethyst, p2 Elite.

Rnds 17–20: K2 Loganberry, p2 Elite.

LAURIE'S CHRYSANTHEMUM MITTENS CHART

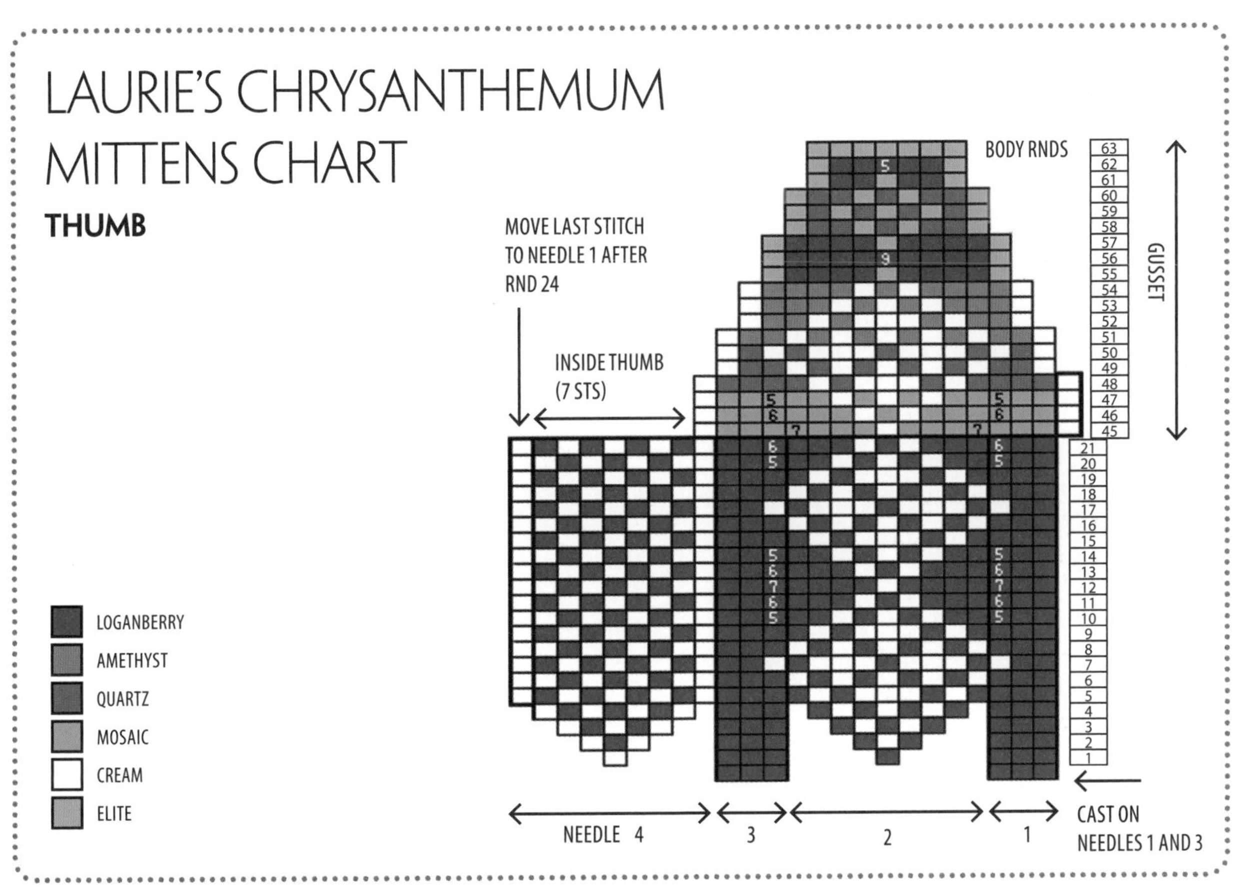

LAURIE'S CHRYSANTHEMUM MITTENS

LAURIE'S CHRYSANTHEMUM MITTENS CHART: **BODY**

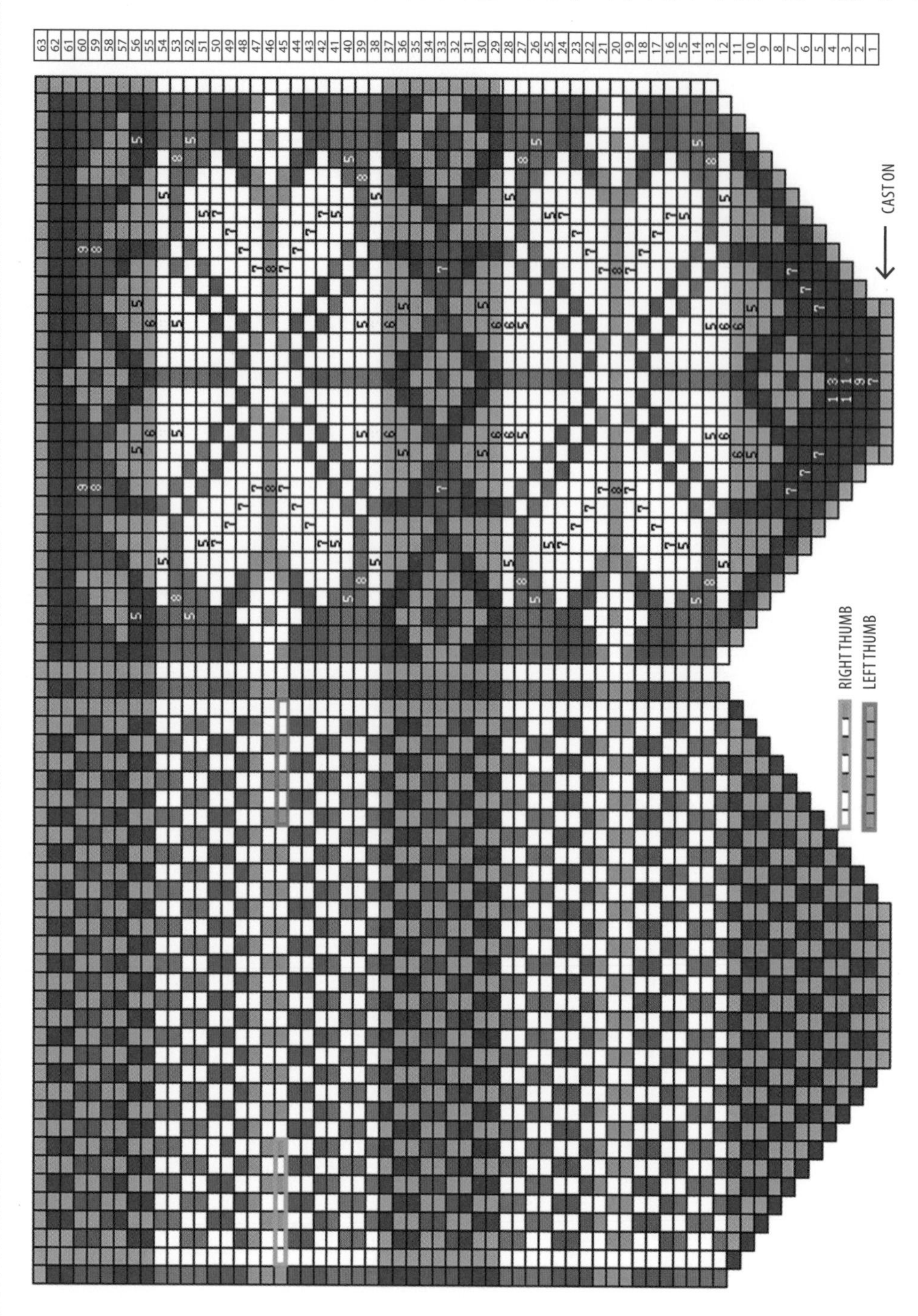

LAURIE'S CHRYSANTHEMUM MITTENS

ALTERNATE COLORWAY

YARN

5 skeins of fingering weight yarn (approx 231yds [211m] per 1.76oz [50g]) in 5 different colors: Black (MC), Blue, Baby Green, Baby Pink and La Vie en Rose

This alternate colorway was made using Cascade Yarns Heritage 150 Solids (merino/nylon, 5.3oz/150g, 492yds/450m) in Black (MC), Araucania Itata Solid (wool/bamboo/silk, 3.5oz/100g, 430yds/393m) in Blue, Baby Green and Baby Pink, and Madelinetosh Tosh Sock (100% merino wool, 4oz/114g, 395yds/361m) in La Vie en Rose.

MITTEN CONSTRUCTION

Follow the general directions through Rnd 61 using Laurie's Chrysanthemum Mittens Charts.

Rnd 62: Follow Laurie's Chrysanthemum Mitten Body Chart.

Rnd 63: Knit with Black while decreasing 6 sts evenly—60 sts.

CUFF

Work 20 rnds using the Corrugated Ribbing Pattern. Bind off in Black.

CORRUGATED RIBBING PATTERN

Rnds 1–4: K2 Black, p2 Blue.

Rnds 5–6: K2 Black, p2 Baby Green.

Rnds 7–8: K2 Black, p2 La Vie en Rose.

Rnds 9–12: K2 Black, p2 Baby Pink.

Rnds 13–14: K2 Black, p2 La Vie en Rose.

Rnds 15–16: K2 Black, p2 Baby Green.

Rnds 17–20: K2 Black, p2 Blue.

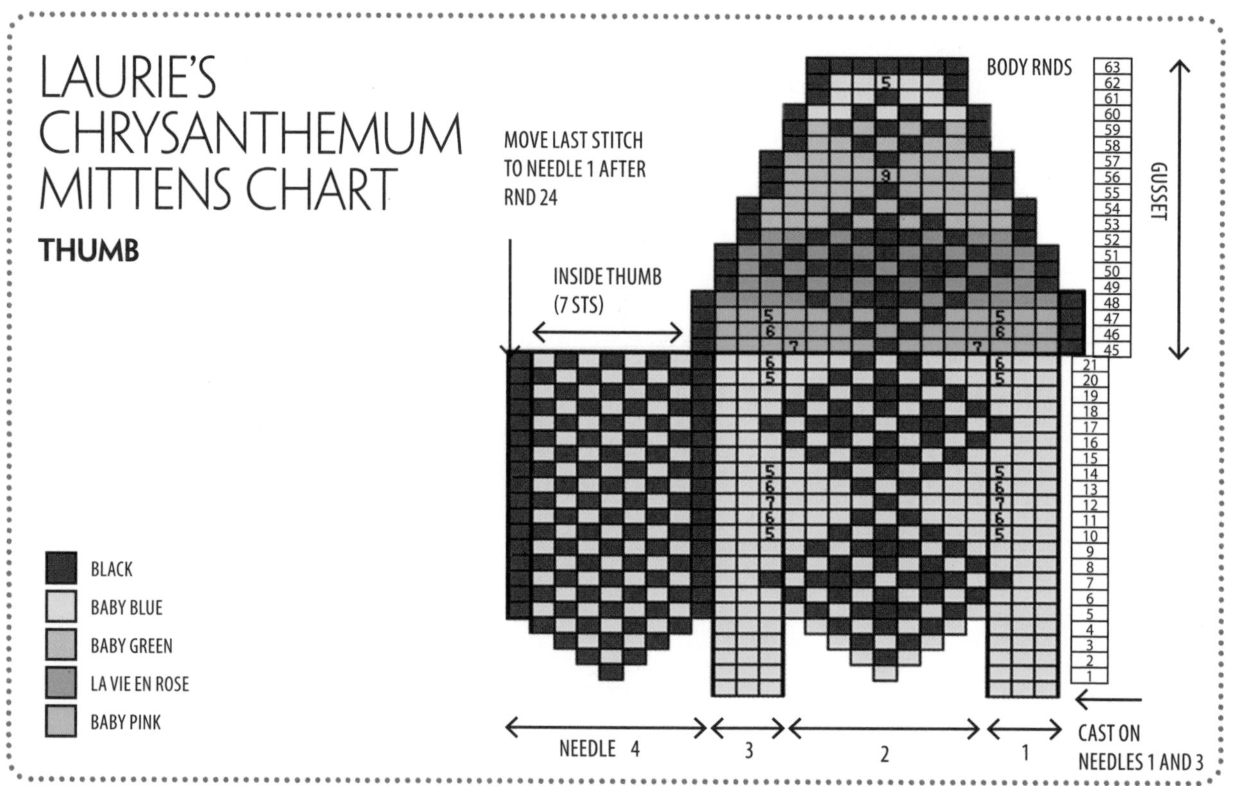

LAURIE'S CHRYSANTHEMUM MITTENS CHART

ALTERNATE COLORWAY - BODY

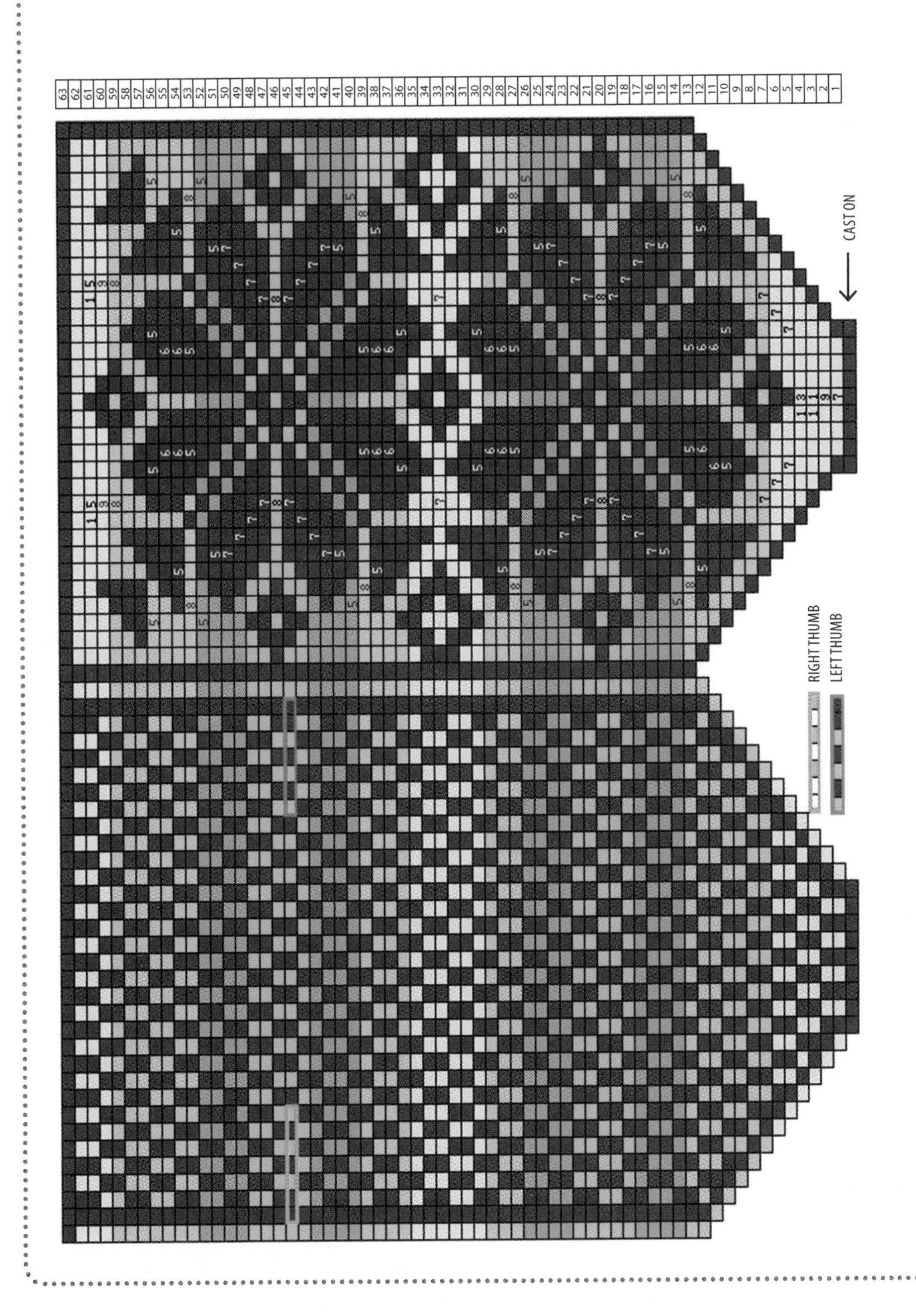

PATTY'S CELTIC CROSS MITTENS

YARN

5 skeins of fingering weight yarn (approx 231yds [211m] per 1.76oz [50g]) in 5 different colors: Oceanic Mix (MC), Turquoise Mix, Redwood Mix, Prune Mix and Natural

The project shown was made using Berroco Ultra Alpaca Fine (alpaca/wool/nylon, 3.5oz/100g, 433yds/396m) in Oceanic Mix, Turquoise Mix, Redwood Mix and Prune Mix, and Knit Picks Bare Gloss Merino Wool/Silk Fingering Weight (merino/silk, 3.5oz/100g, 440yds/402m) in Natural.

MITTEN CONSTRUCTION

Follow the general directions through Rnd 61 using Patty's Celtic Cross Mittens Charts.

Rnd 62: Follow Patty's Celtic Cross Body Chart.

Rnd 63: Knit this rnd with Oceanic Mix while decreasing 6 sts—60 sts.

CUFF

Work 20 rnds using the Corrugated Ribbing Pattern. Bind off in Oceanic Mix.

CORRUGATED RIBBING PATTERN

Rounds 1-4: K2 Oceanic Mix, p2 Natural.

Rounds 5-6: K2 Turquoise Mix, p2 Natural.

Rounds 7-8: K2 Prune Mix, p2 Natural.

Rounds 9-12: K2 Redwood Mix, p2 Natural.

Rounds 13-14: K2 Prune Mix, p2 Natural.

Rounds 15-16: K2 Turquoise Mix, p2 Natural.

Rounds 17-20: K2 Oceanic Mix, p2 Natural.

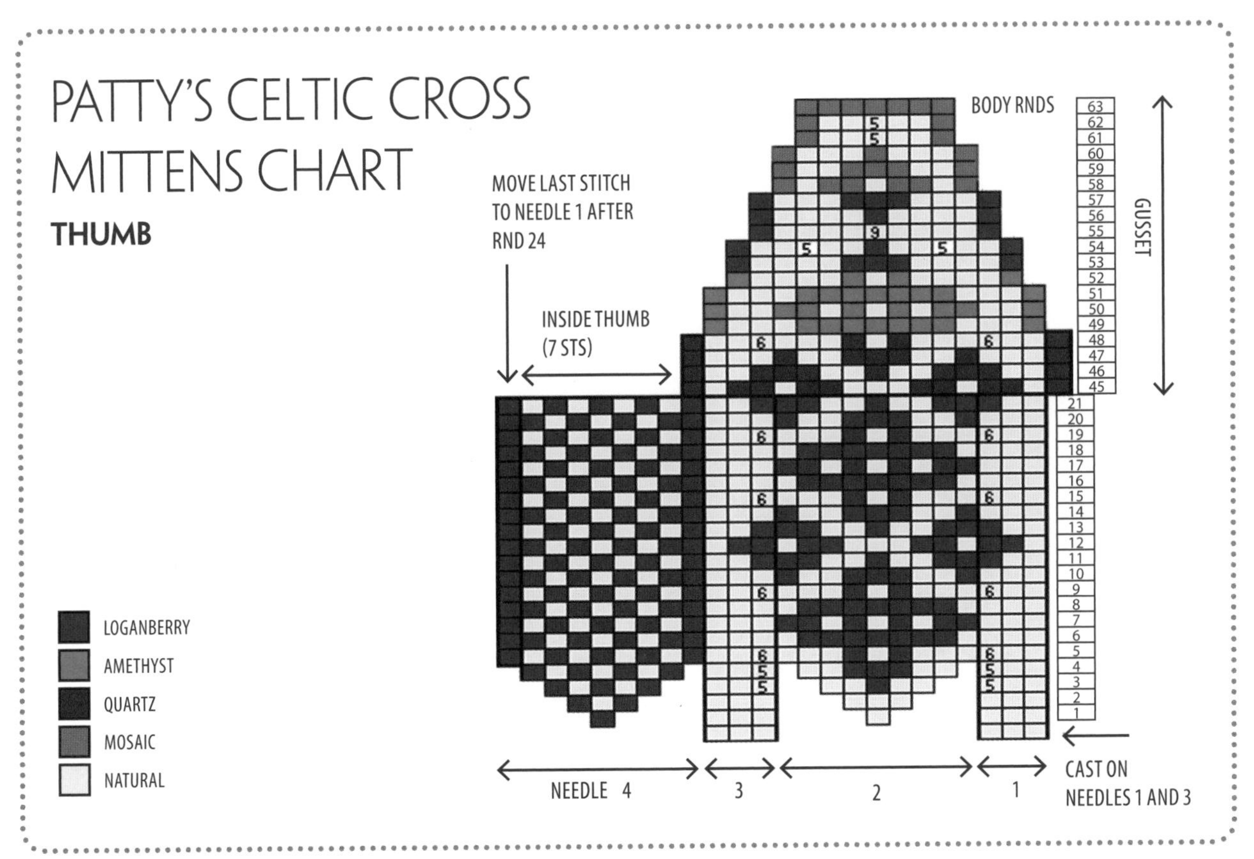

PATTY'S CELTIC CROSS MITTENS

PATTY'S CELTIC CROSS MITTENS CHART: **BODY**

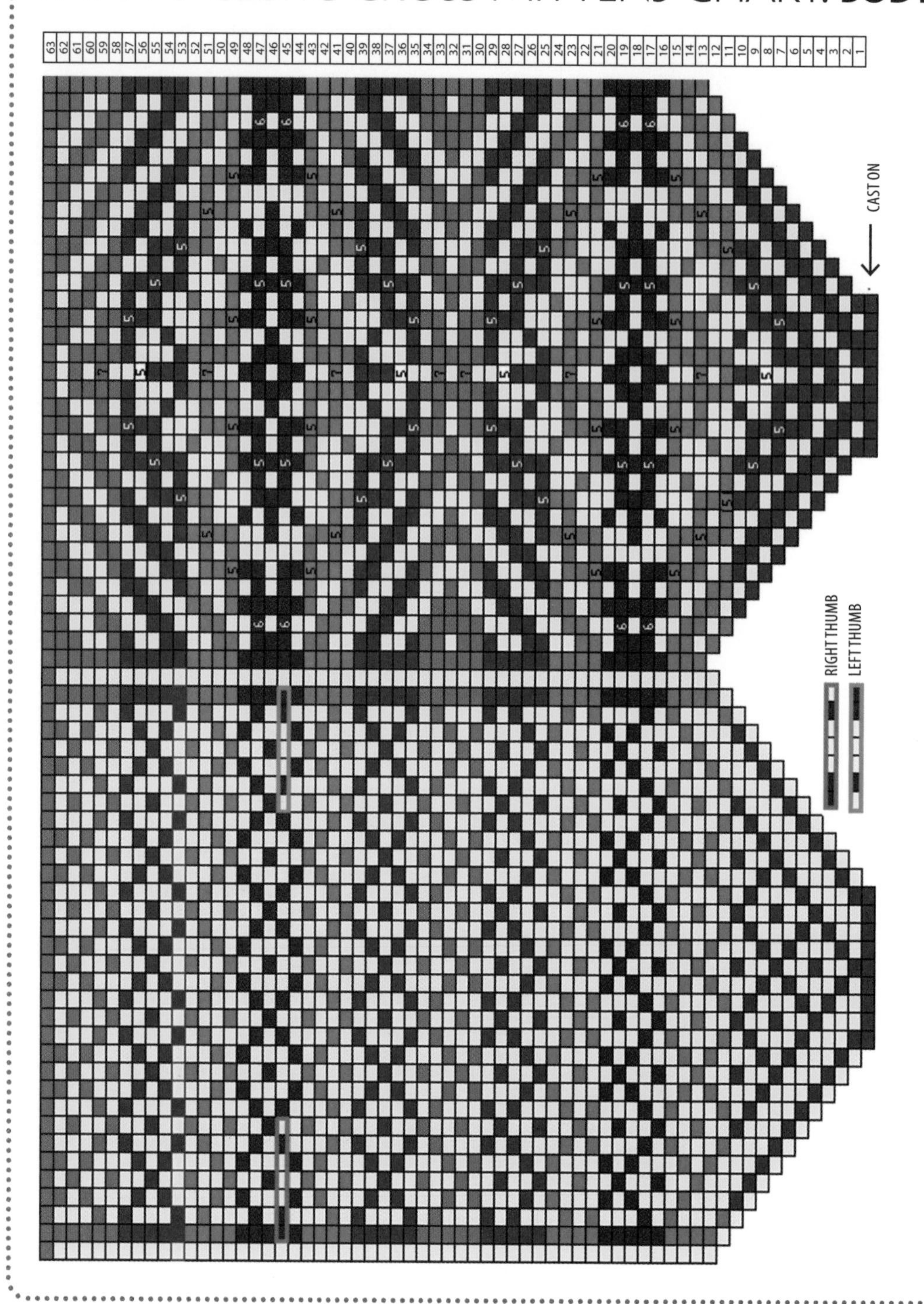

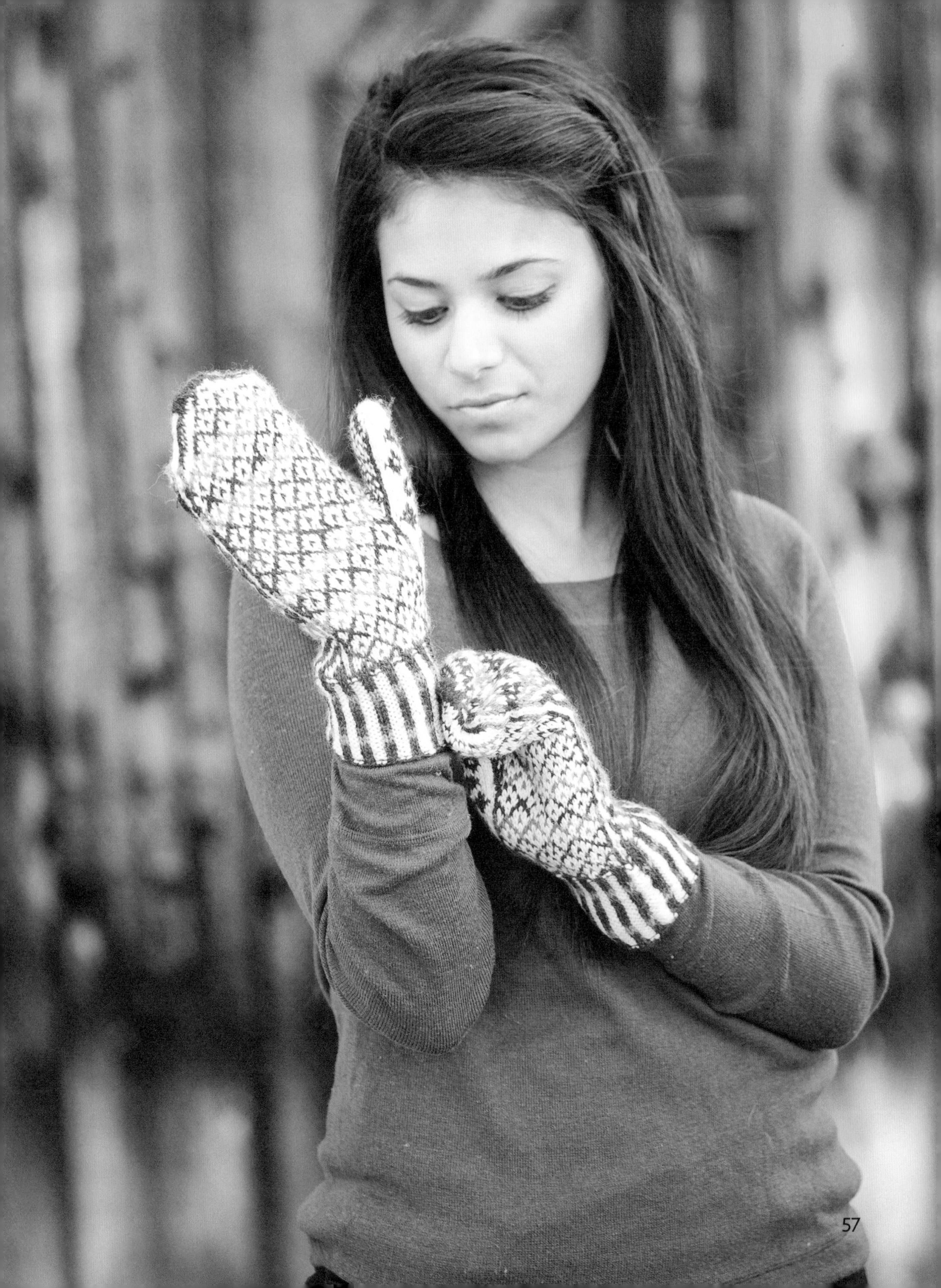

WOMEN'S GLOVES

ANATOMY OF A FINGER-TO-CUFF GLOVE

A finger-to-cuff glove begins with the thumb, which is knit first and placed on safety pins until needed. Next, you will knit the fingers, beginning with the little finger and followed by the ring, middle and index fingers. The little, ring and middle fingers are placed on safety pins until needed for the body. I usually store the glove fingers on a foam core model of my hand. This ensures that the fingers are kept in the correct order.

The fingers and thumbs use a peerie pattern for the back-of-hand side and a salt-and-pepper pattern for the palm side. The peerie patterns for the fingers differ from the pattern for the thumb. All glove finger and thumb patterns are interchangeable. The initial finger and thumb rounds contain the IncR (Increase Right) and IncL (Increase Left) increases.

Once completed, you will join the fingers to construct the glove body. When joining, the peerie patterns should be on the back of the hand and the salt-and-pepper pattern should be on the palm. The glove bodies use a large traditional pattern for the back of the hand and a peerie pattern different from the one used on the fingers and thumb for the palm. The palm patterns are also interchangeable among the gloves.

The glove ends with a cuff of corrugated ribbing. The color sequence is given for each individual glove design.

The glove bodies vary in the number and colors of yarns, the numbers of stitches to increase on Round 1 and occasionally in the total number of rounds. Each pattern contains a color list, ribbing chart, pattern charts, instructions for Round 1 and, if needed, the final rounds. The general directions are given here.

Directions are also included for knitting the gloves from the cuff to the finger for those who prefer this method.

SIZE

One size fits most women

MEASUREMENTS

Length from middle finger to cuff: 9½" (24cm)

Circumference: 7½" (19cm)

NEEDLES

One 6" (15cm) set of US 2 double-pointed needles

One 8" (20.5cm) set of US 2 double-pointed needles

If necessary, change needle size to obtain correct gauge.

NOTIONS

Safety pins

Stitch markers

Tapestry needle

GAUGE

4" (10cm) = 24 sts and 32 rnds in salt-and-pepper pattern.

GLOVE HINTS

Hints for the Glove Body

When beginning the body, the stitches will be stiff on the first two or three rounds because you're changing the shape of the knitting. Don't worry; they loosen up.

Hints for Knitting the Fingers and Thumbs

Although the patterns show four needles in action, I typically use only three for ease in knitting. Feel free to divide the stitches as you see fit.

The initial three rounds are difficult because you have only a few stitches each on four needles. Once you make it past these rounds, the knitting becomes easier.

After Round 10 you might wish to weave the cast-on yarn tail to the inside of the finger or thumb. This not only gets the yarn out of your way, it saves you time later.

Minimizing Holes Between Fingers and Thumbs

You will notice a gap where each finger meets its neighbor and when you attach the thumb where the thumb joins the glove body. To minimize a gap, slip the stitch before the gap. Pick up the left and right stitches one round before the gap. Knit these two stitches together. Pass the slipped stitch over the stitches knit together as you would for sl 1, k2tog, psso. Do this for each side of the finger or thumb. Any remaining gap will be very small and you can use the tail remaining from the 3-Needle Bind Off to close this gap.

FINGER-TO-CUFF GLOVES

Note: All gloves use the same technique for construction. The Fingers and Thumb are knit first and stored until you're ready to construct the glove Body. Each design contains its own Finger and Thumb Charts; however, the charts are interchangeable. This means that you can substitute the Fingers and Thumb from one design into another design.

THUMBS

Using the Turkish cast on (see page 138) and MC, cast on 6 sts onto the 6" (15cm) needles—3 sts on each needle. Knit across the sts on each needle.

Refer to the Thumb Chart for the desired glove design. Because the first rnd contains a single increase, it is easier to combine Needles 1 and 2 onto the first needle and Needles 3 and 4 onto the second needle. This lessens the possibility of the sts slipping off the ends of the needle.

Thumb Rnd 1 (Inc Rnd):

First Needle: Knit the 3 cast-on sts following the pattern for Needle 1. M1, following the pattern for Needle 2.

Second Needle: Knit the 3 cast-on sts following the pattern for Needle 3. M1 following the pattern for Needle 4—8 sts.

On Rnd 2, divide the sts onto 4 needles.

Thumb Rnd 2 (Inc Rnd):

Needle 1: Knit the 3 sts following the pattern for Needle 1—1 st remains on the left needle.

Needle 2: With a new needle, Needle 2, IncR following the pattern for the first stitch on Needle 2. Knit the next stitch following the pattern for Needle 2. IncL following the pattern for the last stitch on Needle 2.

Needle 3: Knit the 3 sts following the pattern for Needle 3—1 st remains on the left needle.

Needle 4: IncR following the pattern for the first stitch on Needle 4. Knit the next stitch following the pattern for Needle 4. IncL following the pattern for the last stitch on Needle 4—12 sts.

Thumb Rnds 3–5 (Inc Rnds): Continue to follow the Thumb Chart for your pattern, increasing 1 st at each end of Needle 2 and Needle 4—24 sts after Rnd 5.

Rnds 6–20: Follow the Thumb Chart.

Rnd 21: Follow the Thumb Chart to the last stitch. Do not knit this stitch. Move the last stitch on Needle 4 onto Needle 1. Similarly, move the first stitch on Needle 4 onto Needle 3—7 sts remain on Needle 4. Place these 7 inside-thumb sts on a safety pin. Divide the remaining 17 sts between 2 safety pins.

FINGERS

Note: All Fingers begin the same way and use the same chart; they are knit to different lengths, indicated on the chart by the number of rows worked for each. Make the Index Finger last, and do not cut the thread.

The right-hand Fingers begin with Needle 1; the left-hand Fingers begin with Needle 3.

Using the Turkish cast on and MC, cast on 6 sts onto 6" (15cm) needles—3 sts on each needle. Knit across the sts on each needle.

Finger Rnd 1 (Inc Rnd):

First Needle: Knit the 3 cast-on sts following the pattern for Needle 1. M1, following the pattern for Needle 2.

Second Needle: Knit the 3 cast-on sts following the pattern for Needle 3. M1, following the pattern for Needle 4—8 sts.

On Rnd 2, divide the sts onto 4 needles.

Finger Rnd 2 (Inc Rnd):

Note: For left hand, begin with Needles 3 and 4 and end with Needles 1 and 2.

Needle 1: Knit the 3 sts following the pattern for Needle 1—1 st remains on the left needle.

Needle 2: With a new needle, Needle 2, IncR following the pattern for the first stitch on Needle 2. Knit the next stitch following the pattern for Needle 2. IncL following the pattern for the last stitch on Needle 2.

Needle 3: Knit the 3 sts following the pattern for Needle 3—1 st remains on the left needle.

Needle 4: IncR following the pattern for the first stitch on Needle 4. Knit the next stitch following the pattern for Needle 4. IncL following the pattern for the last stitch on Needle 4—12 sts.

Finger Rnds 3–4 (Inc Rnds):

Follow the Finger Chart, increasing 1 st at each end of Needle 2 and Needle 4—20 sts after Rnd 4.

Continue to follow the Finger Chart until you have reached the correct number of rnds as indicated by the chart for the Finger you are working on: Pinkie, Ring, Middle or Index.

For all Fingers except the Index Finger, place the sts from each needle on a separate safety pin. Cut the yarns, leaving long tails.

Divide the sts onto safety pins as follows: 3, 7, 3, 7. Set the Fingers aside, placing them on a foam core template if possible.

For the Index Finger, DO NOT CUT THE YARNS. You will use it to start the glove Body.

CONNECTING FINGERS

Once the Fingers and Thumb have been knit for a glove, assemble the glove Body. Beginning with the Little Finger, remove the 3 between-Finger sts from the Little Finger and place them on a 6" (15cm) needle. (The between-finger sts for the Little Finger are those next to the cut yarn.) Remove the 3 between-finger sts from the Ring Finger (the 3 sts opposite the cut yarn). Place these sts on a second 6" (15cm) needle.

Place the right sides of the Little and Ring Fingers together. Make sure that the salt-and-pepper patterns are on one side and the peerie patterns are on the other side. With a yarn tail from the Little Finger, use the 3-Needle Bind Off to secure the 3 Finger sts, but do not cut the yarn when you are finished.

Repeat this procedure to join the Ring Finger to the Middle Finger and the Middle Finger to the Index Finger.

Remove 7 peerie Index Finger sts from the safety pin and place them on an 8" (20.5cm) needle. These will be the 7 sts next to the live yarns. Place the 7 salt-and-pepper Index Finger sts on a second 8" (20.5cm) needle—3 Index Finger sts remain. Divide these sts between the peerie (back-of-hand) and salt-and-pepper (palm) needles as indicated by your design's chart. Remove the adjacent 7 Middle Finger peerie sts and the adjacent 7 peerie Ring Finger sts and place them on the back-of-hand needle. Repeat for the palm sts. Remove the adjacent 7 peerie Little Finger sts and add them to the back-of-hand needle. Remove the adjacent 7 salt-and-pepper Little Finger sts and add them to the palm needle—3 Little Finger sts remain. Divide these between the back-of-hand and palm needles as indicated by your chosen design. Divide the palm sts between 2 needles.

Your chosen design will indicate the number of sts on the back-of-hand side and palm side of the glove.

BODY

The right glove Body is knit from the pattern side to the palm side. The entire Back of Hand pattern is on Needle 1. The Palm Chart is divided between Needles 2 and 3.

The left glove Body is knit from the palm side to the back-of-hand side. The Palm Chart is divided between Needles 1 and 2. The back-of-hand side sts are on Needle 3.

Rnd 1: This rnd is pattern-specific and contains instructions for stitch increases. It is always knit in 1 color because you are also joining the sts to form the glove body. See the hints for minimizing gaps below.

Rnds 2–18: Follow the Back-of-Hand and Palm Charts.

Rnd 19 (Attach Thumb):

Right Glove: Knit to the last 7 sts. Use the 3-Needle Bind Off to bind off the 7 palm sts with the inside-thumb sts. Place the 17 Thumb sts onto the needle. (This will be Needle 3.) Knit the Thumb sts using the Thumb Chart.

Left Glove: Use the 3-Needle Bind Off to bind off the first 7 palm sts with the 7 inside-thumb sts. Place the 17 Thumb sts onto the needle. (This will be Needle 1.) Knit the Thumb sts using the Thumb Chart. Knit the remaining palm sts. Knit the Back-of-Hand Chart.

Rnds 20–34: Continue to follow the Back-of-Hand and Palm Charts, as well as the Thumb Chart.

Ending Rnd(s): Most designs end with Rnd 35. Your chosen design instructions indicate the ending rnds.

CUFF

Follow the Corrugated Ribbing Pattern for your chosen design.

FINISHING

Weave in all ends and block flat.

CUFF-TO-FINGER GLOVES

Note: Both Gloves are knit from the back of the hand to the palm.

CUFF

Cast on 60 sts using the bind-off color. Knit the 20 rnds of Corrugated Ribbing Pattern as specified by your pattern.

BODY (RIGHT GLOVE)

Note: Each glove is knit from the back of the hand to the palm. Turn all charts upside down to reorient them for cuff-up knitting.

On the first pattern rnd, increase the same number of sts as the ribbing decreases. On this rnd, knit the back-of-hand sts following the Back-of-Hand Chart onto Needle 1. Divide the palm and Thumb gusset sts between 2 needles as follows: Knit the first 7 sts following the Thumb Chart, pm. Knit the remaining sts following the Palm Chart; however, begin with the eighth stitch in the chart to ensure that the palms match.

Note: The peerie patterns are typically less than 7 stitches. Count the pattern repeats to figure out the eighth stitch.

Cont to knit each rnd following the Back-of-Hand, Thumb and Palm Charts, until Thumb Chart Rnd 19. Knit this rnd as usual. On the next rnd, knit the back-of-hand sts, place the 17 Thumb sts on a holder and cast on 7 sts. Knit these 7 sts following the Palm Chart. Knit the remaining palm sts.

Continue to knit the Back-of-Hand and Palm Charts through Rnd 2. On Rnd 1, decrease the sts indicated as increases on your glove design.

Note: Finger knitting is easier if you first place the unneeded sts on safety pins as indicted in the directions for finger-to-cuff gloves.

FINGERS (RIGHT GLOVE)

Knit from the Little Finger to the Index Finger. For all Fingers, use this needle sequence: Needle 3 (edge or between-finger sts), Needle 2 (back-of-hand), Needle 1 (edge or between-finger sts), Needle 4 (palm salt-and-pepper pattern).

LITTLE FINGER

Rnd 1 (Rnd 19, Upside Down): Place 7 palm sts and 7 back-of-hand sts from glove needles on two 6" (15cm) needles. Knit in pattern the edge sts (Needle 3) as indicated in the glove construction section. Knit 7 back-of-hand sts following the Finger Chart. Cast on 3 sts following Needle 1 of the Finger Chart. Knit 7 palm sts following the Finger Chart.

Rnds 18–4: Knit the sts following the Finger Chart.

Rnd 3: *K3 in pattern, sl 1, k1, psso, k3 in pattern, k2tog. Repeat from * twice.

Rnd 2: *K3 in pattern, sl 1, k1, psso, k1 in pattern, k2tog. Repeat from * twice.

Rnd 1: *K3 in pattern, sl 1, k2tog, psso, k3 in pattern, k2tog. Repeat from * twice.

Last Rnd: K2 in pattern, sl 1, k1, psso, k2 in pattern, k2tog. Draw remaining threads through in loop with MC.

RING FINGER

Rnd 1 (Rnd 23, Upside Down): Place 7 palm sts and 7 back-of-hand sts from glove onto two 6" (15cm) needles. Beginning at Needle 3 of the Finger Chart, pick up and knit 3 between-Finger sts from the Little Finger edge. Knit 7 back-of-hand sts following the Finger Chart. Cast on 3 sts following the Finger Chart. Knit 7 palm sts following the Finger Chart.

Rnds 22–4: Follow the Finger Chart.

Rnds 3 to Last Rnd: Follow the Little Finger instructions.

MIDDLE FINGER

Rnd 1 (Rnd 25, Upside Down): Place 7 palm sts and 7 back-of-hand sts from glove onto two 6" (15cm) needles. Beginning at Needle 3 of the Finger Chart, pick up and knit 3 between-finger sts from the Ring Finger edge. Knit 7 back-of-hand sts following the Finger Chart. Cast on 3 sts the following Finger Chart. Knit 7 palm sts the following Finger Chart.

Rnds 24–4: Follow the Finger Chart.

Rnds 3 to Last Rnd: Follow the Little Finger instructions.

INDEX FINGER

Rnd 1 (Rnd 21, Upside Down): Place 7 palm sts and 7 back-of-hand sts from glove onto two 6" (15cm) needles. Beginning at Needle 3 of the Finger Chart, pick up and knit 3 between-finger sts from the Middle Finger edge. Knit 7 back-of-hand sts following the Finger Chart. Place 3 edge sts on a needle as indicated in your chosen design's instructions and knit following the Finger Chart. Knit 7 palm sts following the Finger Chart.

Rnds 20–4: Follow the Finger Chart.

Rnds 3 to Last Rnd: Follow the Little Finger directions.

THUMB

Remove the 17 Thumb sts from the holder and divide between 2 needles. The first and last sts will be placed with the Needle 4 sts. To do this, move the leftmost Thumb stitch to a new needle. Knit this stitch following the Thumb Chart, then pick up and knit 7 sts following Needle 4 of the Thumb Chart. (This is your rnd start.) Knit the next stitch onto Needle 4. Knit the remaining Thumb sts following the Thumb Chart.

Knit the Thumb Chart until Rnd 4.

Rnds 4, 3 and 2 Decreases: Sl 1, k1, psso, knit in pattern to the last two Needle 4 sts, k2tog, sl 1, k1, psso, knit in pattern to the last 5 sts, k2tog, knit remaining 3 sts in pattern.

Rnd 1 Decreases: *Sl 1, k2tog, psso, k3 in pattern. Repeat from * twice.

Last Dec Rnd: Move 1 remaining Needle 3 stitch to Needle 1, k2tog, k2 in pattern, sl 1, k1, psso, knit to end of rnd. Cut yarns. Draw remaining sts through with a loop and secure or Kitchener stitch them.

BODY (LEFT GLOVE)

On the first pattern rnd, increase the same number of sts as the ribbing decreases. On this rnd, knit the back-of-hand sts onto Needle 1. Divide the palm and Thumb gusset sts between 2 needles as follows: Knit the palm pattern to the last 7 sts, pm, knit the remaining 7 sts following the Thumb gusset pattern.

Cont to knit each rnd following the Back-of-Hand, Palm and Thumb Charts until Thumb Chart Rnd 19. Knit this rnd as usual. On the next rnd, knit the Back-of-Hand and Palm Charts to the Thumb gusset. Place the 17 Thumb gusset sts on a holder, and cast on 7 sts. Knit these 7 sts following the Palm Chart.

Continue to knit the Back-of-Hand and Palm Charts through Rnd 2. On Rnd 1, decrease the sts indicated as increases on your glove pattern.

FINGERS (LEFT GLOVE)

The left glove Fingers follow the same directions as the right glove Fingers; however, knit the Fingers from the Index Finger to the Little Finger.

Knit the Thumb using the right glove directions.

FINISHING

Turn the glove inside out and weave in all ends. Block.

JENNY'S MAZE GLOVES

JENNY'S MAZE GLOVES

YARN

6 skeins of fingering weight yarn (approx 231yds [211m] per 1.76oz [50g]) in 6 different colors: Jay, Eggplant, Regal, Mist, Pennyroyal and Oyster Heather

The project shown on page 64 was made using Knit Picks Palette (100% Peruvian Highland wool, 1.76oz/50g, 231yds/211m) in Jay, Eggplant, Regal, Mist, Pennyroyal and Oyster Heather.

CORRUGATED RIBBING PATTERN

Rnds 1–4: K2 Jay, p2 Mist.

Rnds 5–8: K2 Eggplant, p2 Pennyroyal.

Rnds 9–12: K2 Regal, p2 Oyster Heather.

Rnds 13–16: K2 Eggplant, p2 Pennyroyal.

Rnds 17–20: K2 Jay, p2 Mist.

JENNY'S MAZE GLOVES CHART

FINGER

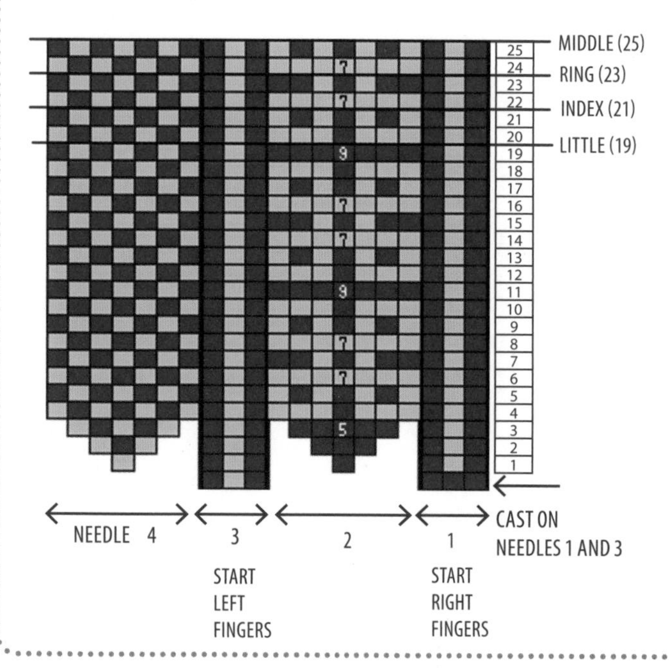

GLOVE CONSTRUCTION

Note: For each glove, the palm contains the 28 palm-side sts. The back-of-hand side contains the 28 sts from the Finger fronts plus the 3 edge sts each from the Index Finger and the Little Finger (34 sts)—62 sts.

Rnd 1: Knit this rnd in Jay. Increase 3 sts evenly on the back-of-hand side and decrease 1 st on the palm side—37 back-of-hand side sts and 27 palm-side sts—64 sts.

Rnds 3–33: Follow the general directions for gloves as well as the Palm, Thumb and Back-of-Hand Charts for Jenny's Maze Gloves.

Rnds 23, 26 and 29 Thumb Decreases: Work decreases as k2tog, work in pattern to the last 2 sts, sl 1, k1, psso.

Rnds 2, 34–35: Knit with Jay.

CUFF

Work 20 rnds using the Corrugated Ribbing Pattern. On the first rnd of ribbing decrease 3 sts on the maze side and 1 st on the palm side—60 sts. Bind off with Jay.

JENNY'S MAZE GLOVES CHART

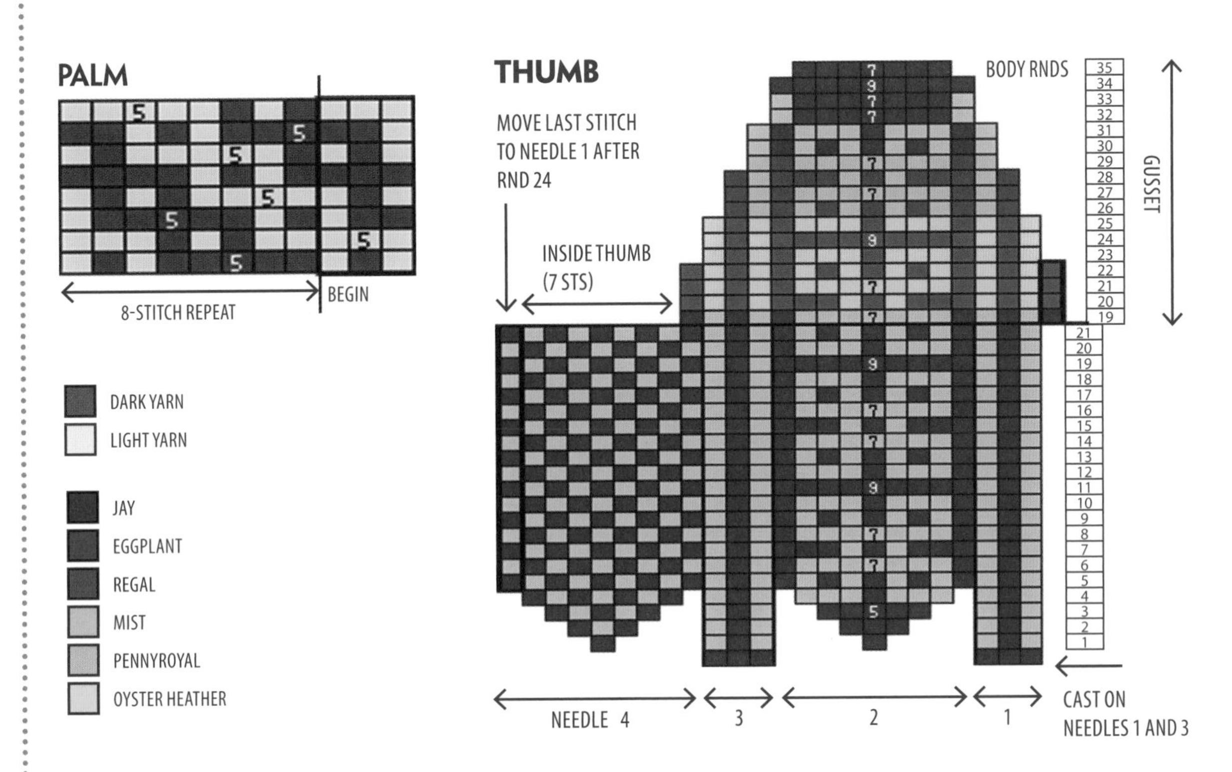

BACK OF HAND

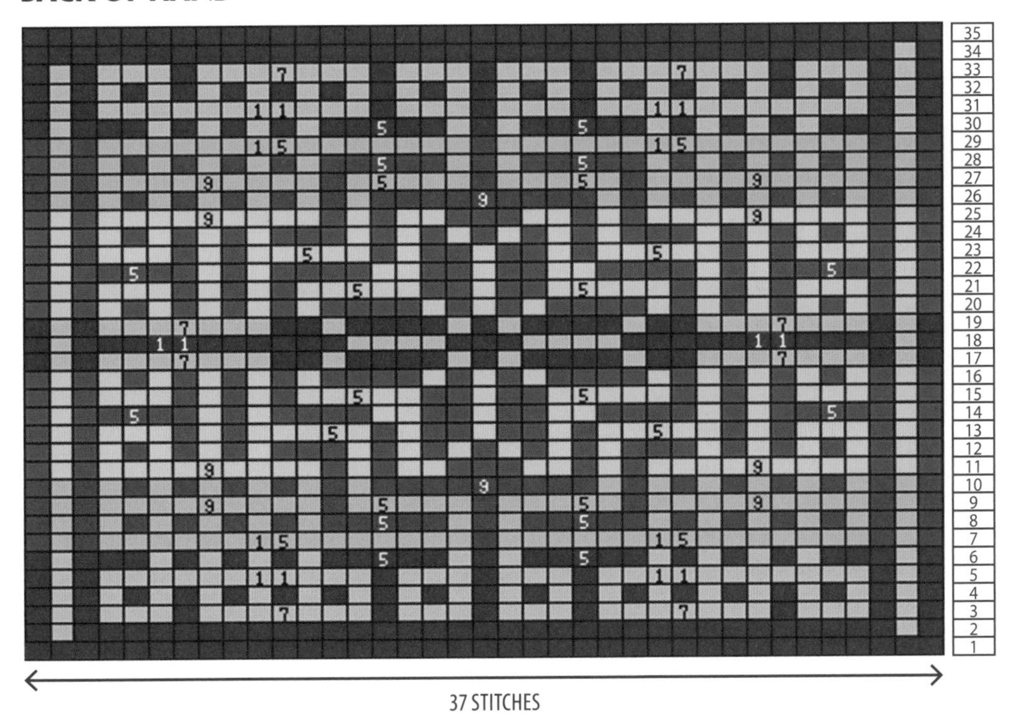

JENNY'S MAZE GLOVES

ALTERNATE COLORWAY

YARN

6 skeins of fingering weight yarn (approx 231yds [211m] per 1.76oz [50g]) in 6 different colors: Mare (MC), Charcoal, Fig, Nectar, Latte and Snow

This alternate colorway was made using Madelinetosh Tosh Merino Light (100% merino wool, 3.5oz/100g, 420yds/384m) in Mare, Charcoal and Fig, Madelinetosh Tosh Sock (100% merino wool, 4oz/114g, 395yds/361m) in Nectar, Araucania Itata Solid (wool/bamboo/silk, 3.5oz/100g, 430yds/393m) in Latte, and Cascade Yarns Heritage 150 Solids (merino/nylon, 5.3oz/150g, 492yds/450m) in Snow.

CORRUGATED RIBBING PATTERN

Rnds 1–4: K2 Mare, p2 Nectar.

Rnds 5–8: K2 Fig, p2 Latte.

Rnds 9–12: K2 Charcoal, p2 Snow.

Rnds 13–16: K2 Fig, p2 Latte.

Rnds 17–20: K2 Mare, p2 Nectar.

JENNY'S MAZE GLOVES CHART

ALTERNATE COLORWAY - FINGER

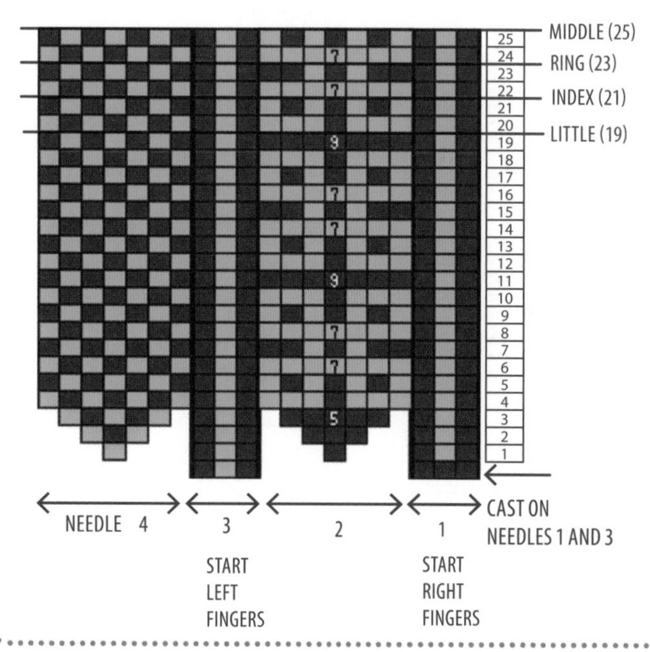

GLOVE CONSTRUCTION

Note: For each glove, the palm contains the 28 palm-side sts. The back-of-hand side contains the 28 sts from the Finger fronts plus the 3 edge sts each from the Index Finger and the Little Finger (34 sts)—62 sts.

Rnd 1: Knit this rnd in Mare. Increase 3 sts evenly on the back-of-hand side and decrease 1 st on the palm side—37 back-of-hand side sts and 27 palm-side sts—64 sts.

Rnds 3–33: Follow the general directions for gloves as well as the Palm, Thumb and Back-of-Hand Charts for Jenny's Maze Gloves.

Rnds 23, 26 and 29 Thumb Decreases: Work decreases as k2tog, work in pattern to the last 2 sts, sl 1, k1, psso.

Rnds 2, 34–35: Knit with Mare.

CUFF

Work 20 rnds using the Corrugated Ribbing Pattern. On the first rnd of ribbing decrease 3 sts on the maze side and 1 st on the palm side—60 sts. Bind off with Mare.

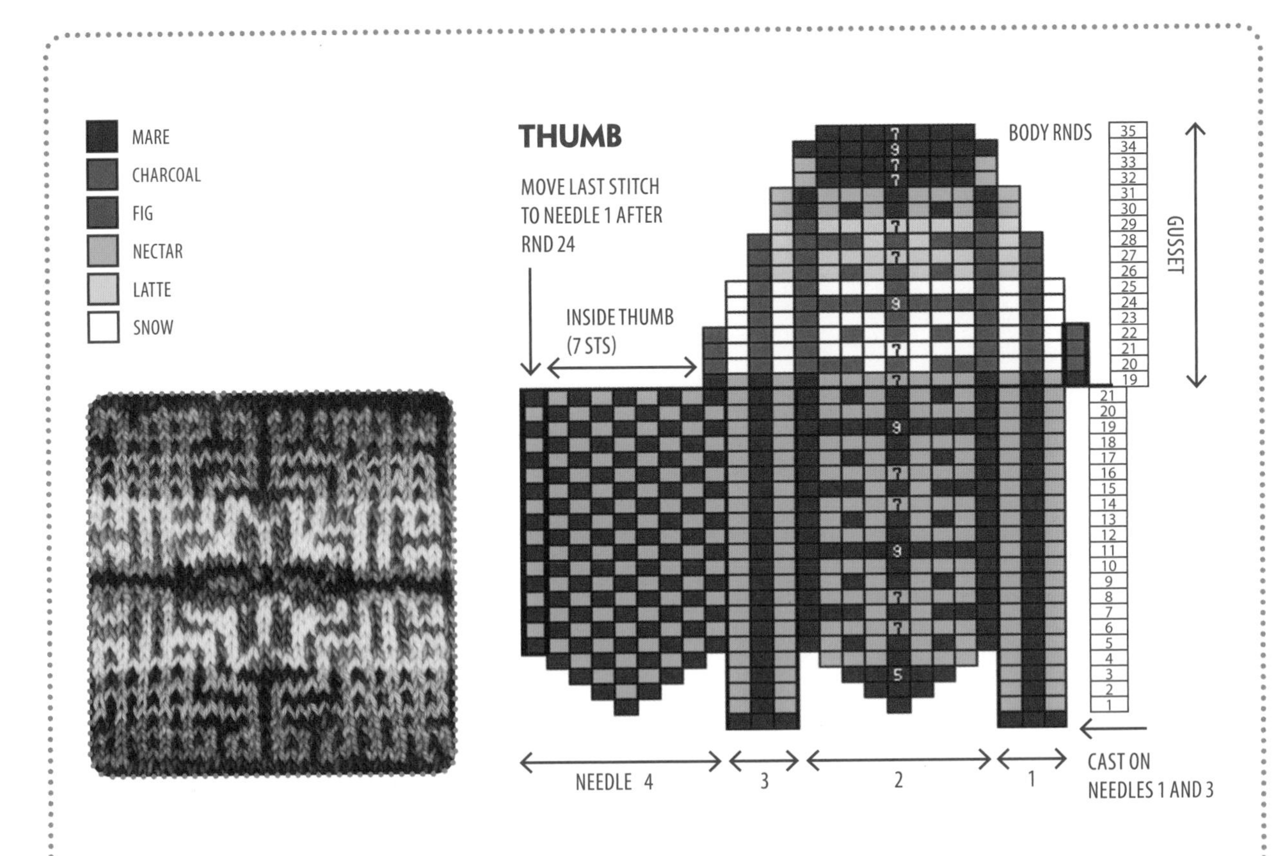
MARE
CHARCOAL
FIG
NECTAR
LATTE
SNOW
THUMB
MOVE LAST STITCH TO NEEDLE 1 AFTER RND 24
INSIDE THUMB (7 STS)
BODY RNDS
GUSSET
NEEDLE 4
3
2
1
CAST ON NEEDLES 1 AND 3

BACK OF HAND

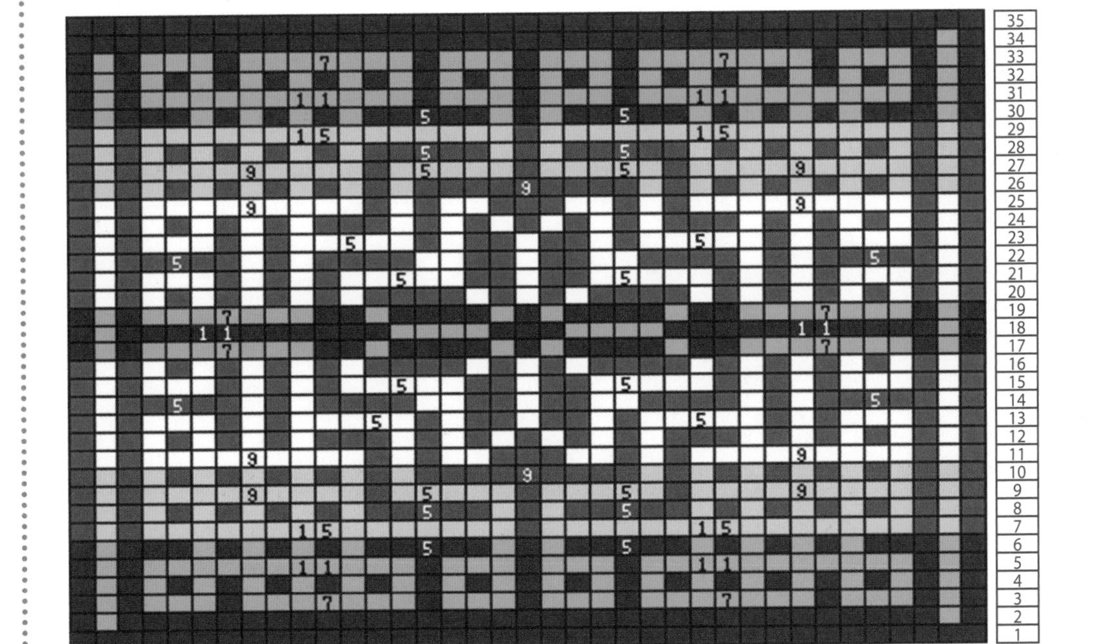
37 STITCHES

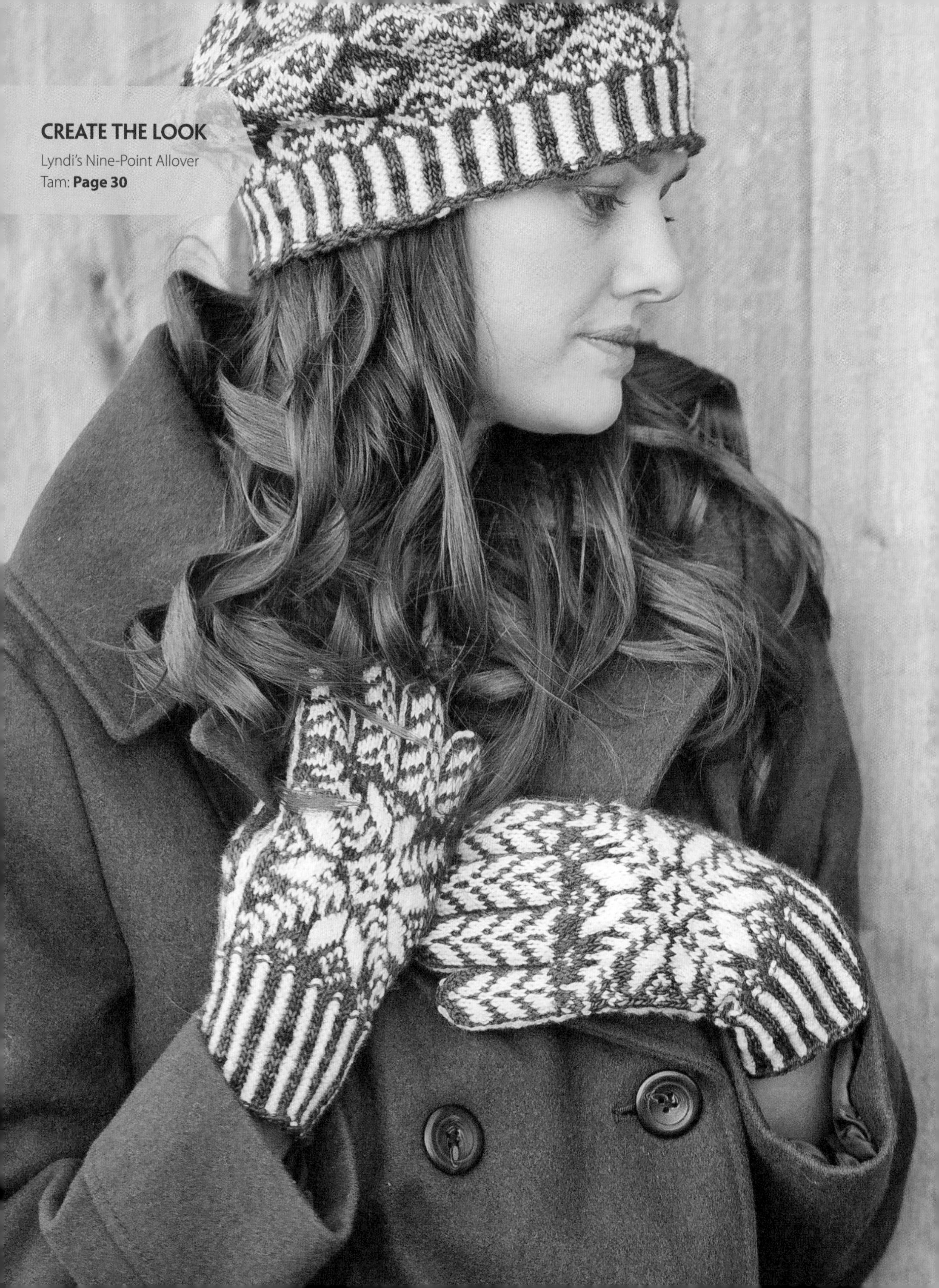

CREATE THE LOOK

Lyndi's Nine-Point Allover Tam: **Page 30**

LYNDI'S FEATHERED STAR GLOVES

YARN

5 skeins of fingering weight yarn (approx 231yds [211m] per 1.76oz [50g]) in 5 different colors: Turquoise, Nebula, Forestry, Jade and Natural

The project shown was made using Cascade Yarns Heritage Silk (merino/silk, 3.5oz/100g, 437yds/400m) in Turquoise, Madelinetosh Tosh Merino Light (100% merino wool, 3.5oz/100g, 420yds/384m) in Nebula, Forestry and Jade, and Knit Picks Bare Stroll Fingering Sock (superwash merino/nylon, 3.5oz/100g, 462yds/422m) in Natural.

LYNDI'S FEATHERED STAR GLOVES CHART

FINGER

TURQUOISE
NEBULA
FORESTRY
JADE
NATURAL

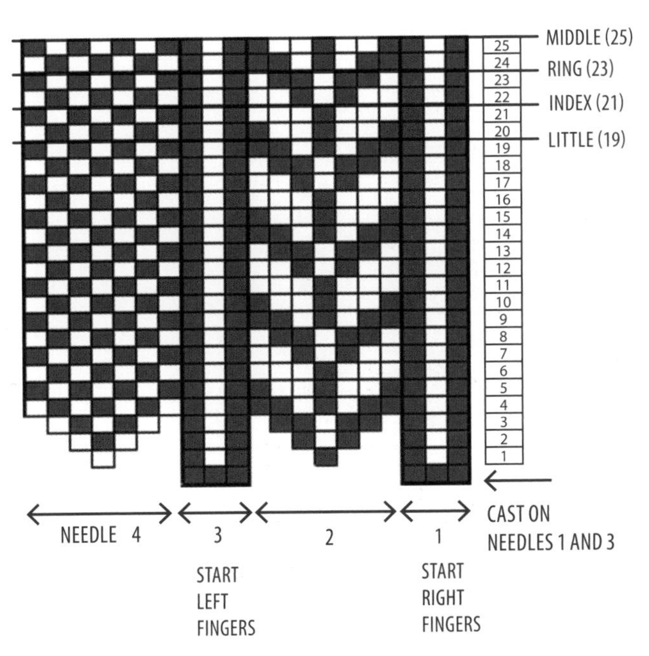

CORRUGATED RIBBING PATTERN

Rnds 1–2: K2 Turquoise, p2 Natural.

Rnds 3–5: K2 Nebula, p2 Natural.

Rnds 6–8: K2 Forestry, p2 Natural.

Rnds 9–12: K2 Jade, p2 Natural.

Rnds 13–15: K2 Forestry, p2 Natural.

Rnds 16–18: K2 Nebula, p2 Natural.

Rnds 19–20: K2 Turquoise, p2 Natural.

GLOVE CONSTRUCTION

Note: For each glove, the palm contains the 28 sts from the palm side of the fingers plus 2 edge sts each from the Index and Little Fingers—32 sts. The back-of-hand side contains the 28 stitches from the front side of the Fingers as well as the 1 remaining edge stitch from the Little Finger and the Index Finger (30 sts)—62 sts.

Rnd 1: Knit this rnd with Turquoise and slip the first and last stitch to maintain the vertical stripe. Increase 5 sts evenly on the back-of-hand side—(37 back-of-hand side sts, 30 palm-side sts)—67 sts.

Rnds 2–35: Follow the general directions for gloves as well as the Palm, Thumb and Back-of-Hand Charts for Lyndi's Feathered Star Gloves.

CUFF

Work 20 rnds using the Corrugated Ribbing Pattern. On the first rnd of ribbing, decrease 4 sts evenly on the star side and 3 sts evenly on the palm side—60 sts. Bind off with Turquoise.

LYNDI'S FEATHERED STAR GLOVES

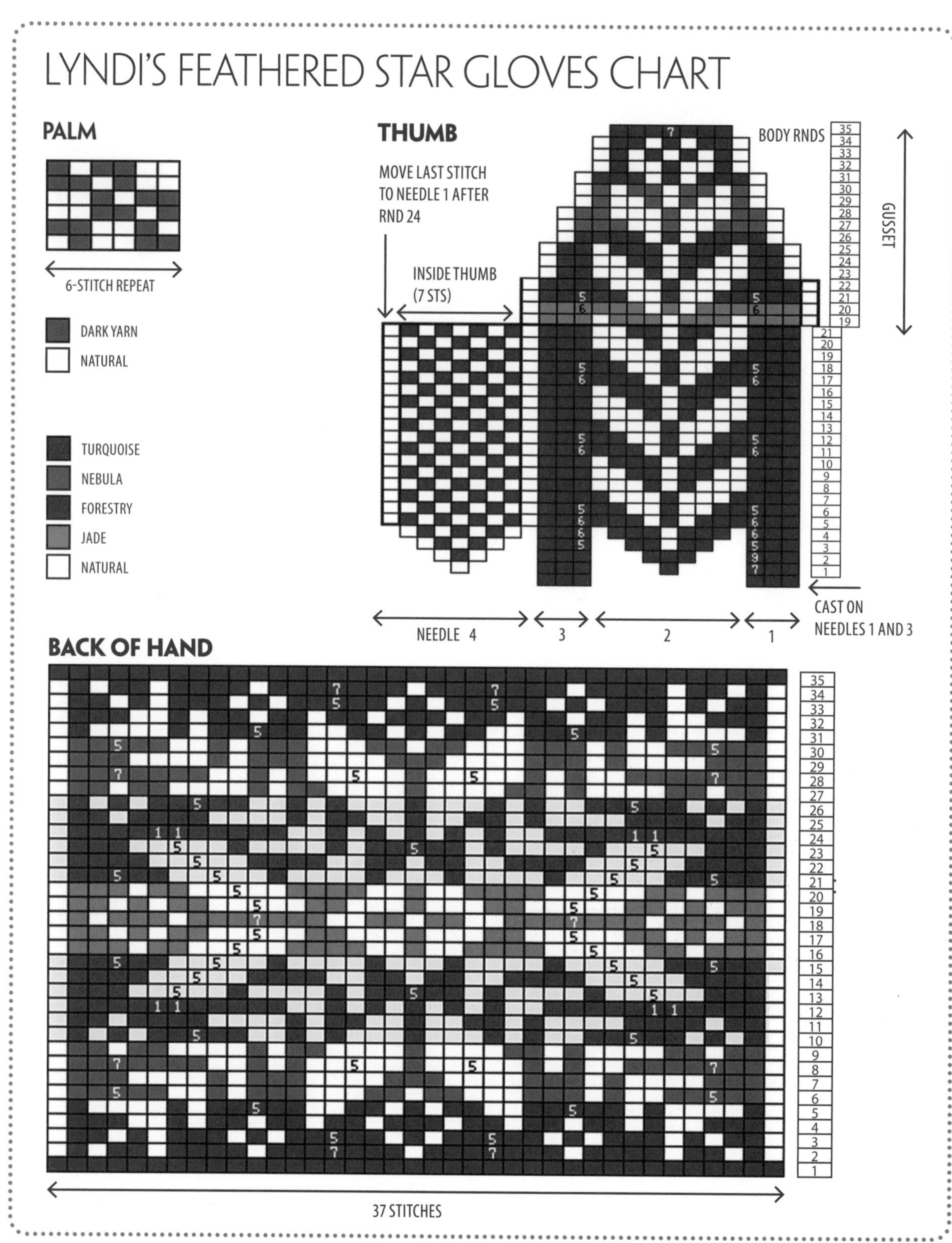

LYNDI'S FEATHERED STAR GLOVES

ALTERNATE COLORWAY

YARN

5 skeins of fingering weight yarn (approx 231yds [211m] per 1.76oz [50g]) in 5 different colors: Tart (MC), Holly Berry, Byzantine, Bronze and Snow

This alternate colorway was made using Madelinetosh Tosh Sock (100% merino wool, 4oz/114g, 395yds/361m) in Tart, Madelinetosh Tosh Merino Light (100% merino wool, 3.5oz/100g, 420yds/384m) in Byzantine, The Alpaca Yarn Company Glimmer (alpaca/polyester, 1.76oz/50g, 183yds/167m) in Holly Berry and Bronze, and Cascade Yarns Heritage 150 Solids (merino/nylon, 5.3oz/150g, 492yds/450m) in Snow.

CORRUGATED RIBBING PATTERN

Rnds 1–2: K2 Tart, p2 Snow.

Rnds 3–5: K2 Holly Berry, p2 Snow.

Rnds 6–8: K2 Byzantine, p2 Snow.

Rnds 9–12: K2 Bronze, p2 Snow.

Rnds 13–15: K2 Byzantine, p2 Snow.

Rnds 16–18: K2 Holly Berry, p2 Snow.

Rnds 19–20: K2 Tart, p2 Snow.

LYNDI'S FEATHERED STAR GLOVES CHART

ALTERNATE COLORWAY - FINGER

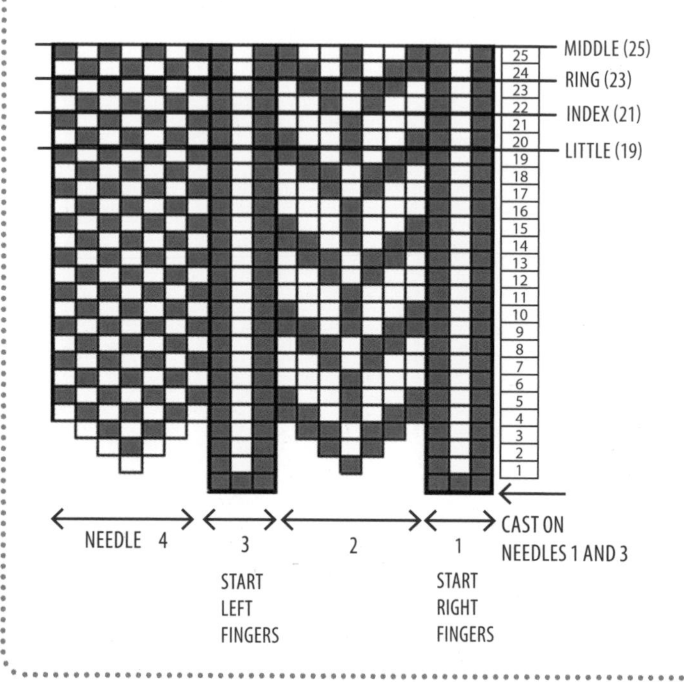

GLOVE CONSTRUCTION

Note: For each glove, the palm contains the 28 sts from the palm side of the fingers plus 2 edge sts each from the Index and Little Fingers—32 sts. The back-of-hand side contains the 28 stitches from the front side of the Fingers as well as the 1 remaining edge stitch from the Little Finger and the Index Finger (30 sts)—62 sts.

Rnd 1: Knit this rnd with Tart and slip the first and last stitch to maintain the vertical stripe. Increase 5 sts evenly on the back-of-hand side—(37 back-of-hand side sts, 30 palm-side sts)—67 sts.

Rnds 2–35: Follow the general directions for gloves as well as the Palm, Thumb and Back-of-Hand Charts for Lyndi's Feathered Star Gloves.

CUFF

Work 20 rnds using the Corrugated Ribbing Pattern. On the first rnd of ribbing, decrease 4 sts evenly on the star side and 3 sts evenly on the palm side—60 sts. Bind off with Tart.

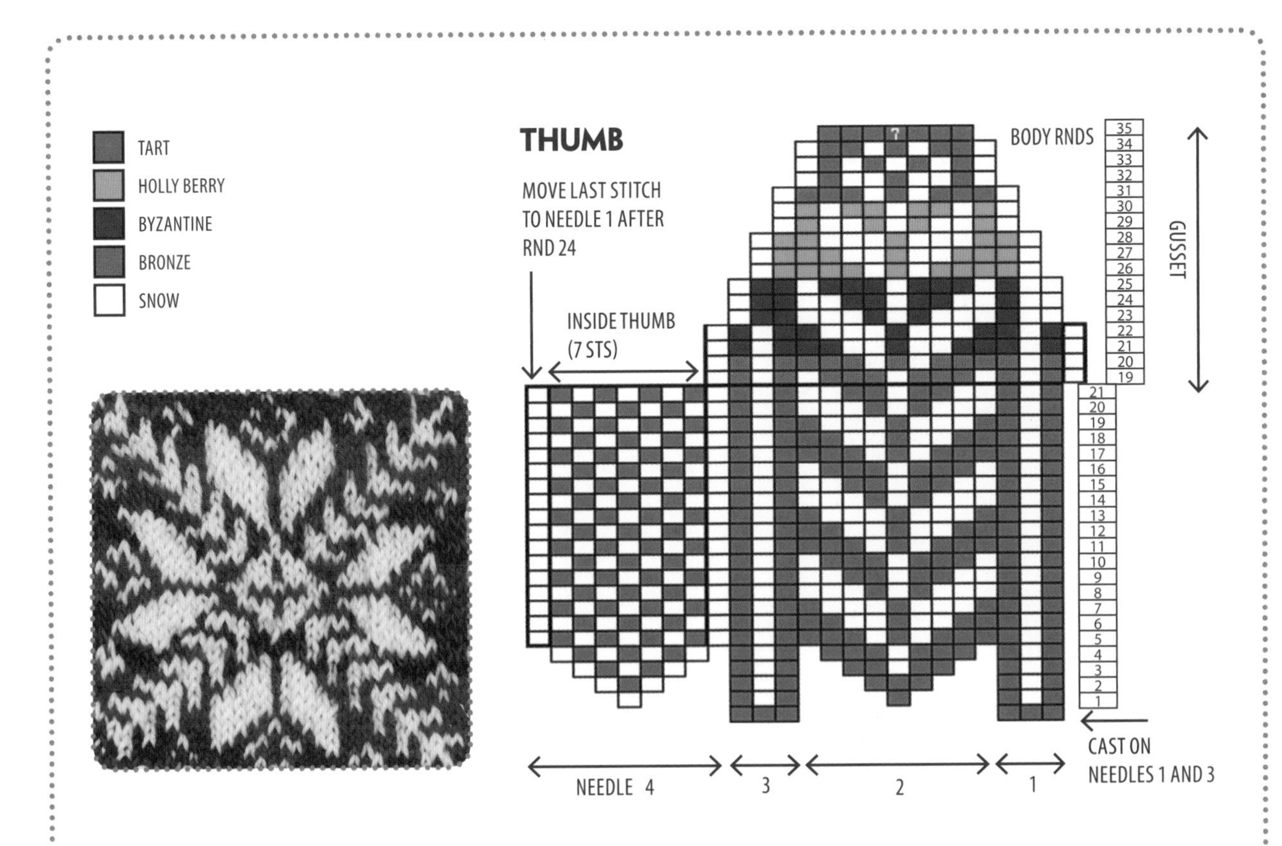
TART
HOLLY BERRY
BYZANTINE
BRONZE
SNOW
THUMB
MOVE LAST STITCH TO NEEDLE 1 AFTER RND 24
INSIDE THUMB (7 STS)
BODY RNDS
GUSSET
CAST ON NEEDLES 1 AND 3
NEEDLE 4
3
2
1

BACK OF HAND

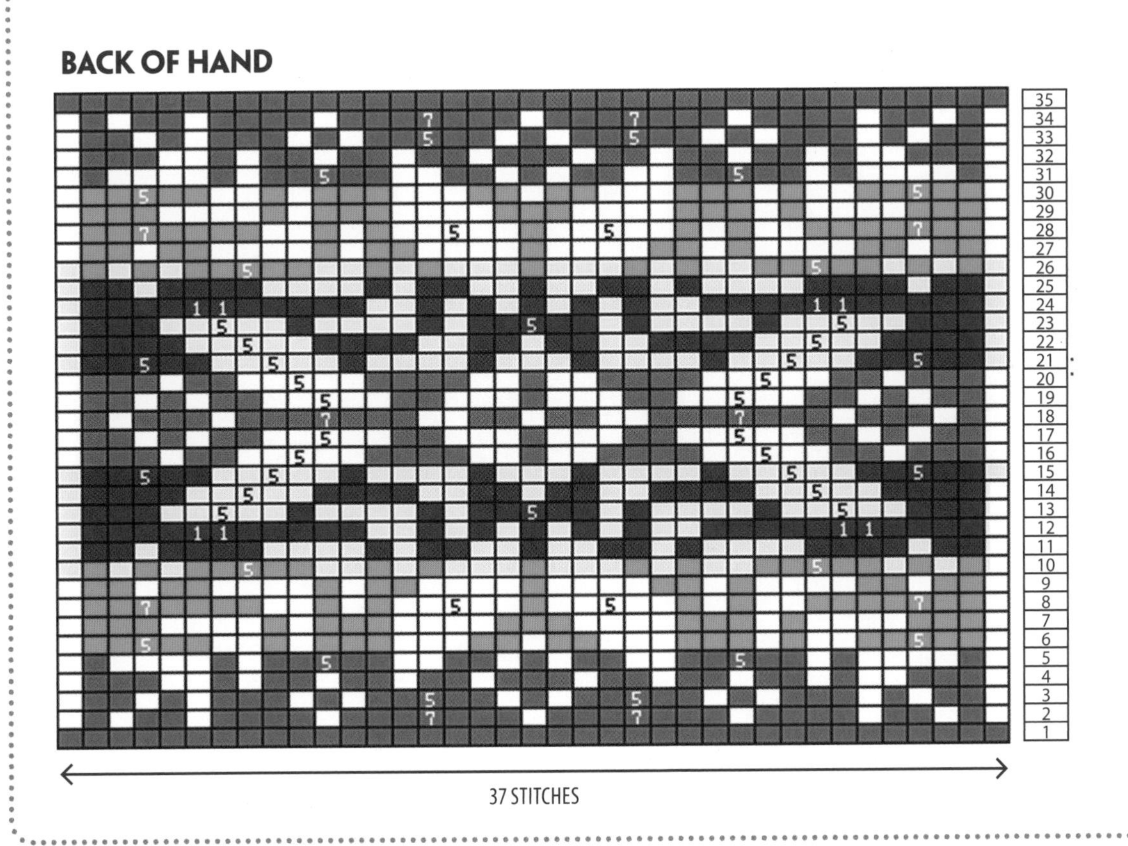
37 STITCHES

SABRINA'S OJO DE DIOS GLOVES

YARN

6 skeins of fingering weight yarn (approx 231 yds [211m] per 1.76oz [50g]) in 6 different colors: Black (MC), Blue, Creme de Menthe, La Vie en Rose, Coral Rose and Pink

The project shown was made using Araucania Ranco Solid (wool/nylon, 3.5oz/100g, 376yds/344m) in Black and Blue, Madelinetosh Tosh Sock (100% merino wool, 4oz/114g, 395yds/361m) in Creme de Menthe and La Vie en Rose, Rio de la Plata Yarns Sock Solid (100% merino wool, 3.5oz/100g, 437yds/400m) in Coral Rose and Araucania Itata Solid (wool/bamboo/silk, 3.5oz/100g, 430yds/393m) in Pink.

SABRINA'S OJO DE DIOS GLOVES CHART

FINGER

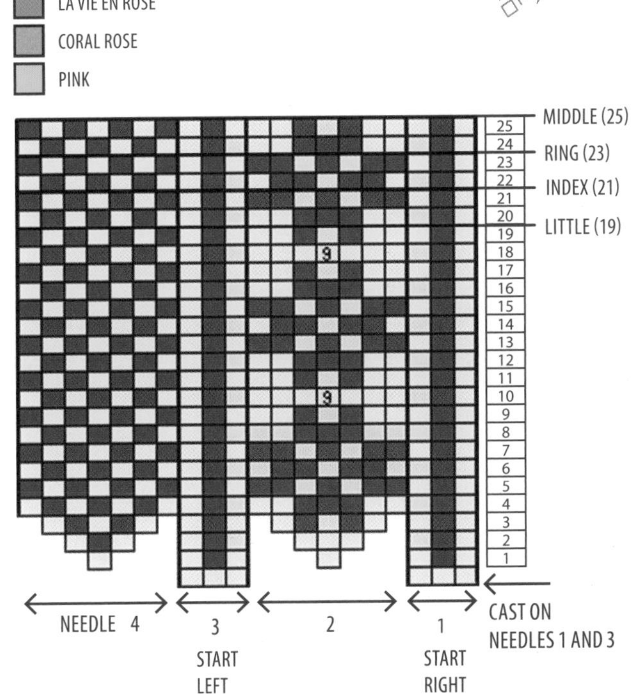

CORRUGATED RIBBING PATTERN

Rnds 1–2: K2 Black, p2 Blue.

Rnds 3–4: K2 Black, p2 La Vie en Rose.

Rnds 5–6: K2 Black, p2 Creme de Menthe.

Rnds 7–8: K2 Black, p2 Pink.

Rnds 9–12: K2 Black, p2 Coral Rose.

Rnds 13–14: K2 Black, p2 Pink.

Rnds 15–16: K2 Black, p2 Creme de Menthe.

Rnds 17–18: K2 Black, p2 La Vie en Rose.

Rnds 19–20: K2 Black, p2 Blue.

GLOVE CONSTRUCTION

Note: For each glove, the palm contains the 28 sts from the palm side of the fingers. The back-of-hand side contains the 28 sts from the fronts of the fingers as well as the 3 edge sts from the Little Finger and the Index Finger (34 sts)—62 sts.

Rnd 1: Knit this rnd with Black. Increase 3 sts evenly on the back-of-hand side and 1 st on the palm side—(37 back-of-hand side sts and 29 palm-side sts)—66 sts.

Rnds 2-35: Follow the general directions for gloves as well as the Palm, Thumb and Back-of-Hand Charts for Sabrina's Ojo de Dios Gloves.

Rnd 35: Knit with Black.

CUFF

Work 20 rnds using the Corrugated Ribbing Pattern. On the first rnd, decrease 4 sts evenly on the Ojo de Dios side and 2 sts evenly on the palm side—60 sts. Bind off with Black.

SABRINA'S OJO DE DIOS GLOVES

SABRINA'S OJO DE DIOS GLOVES CHART

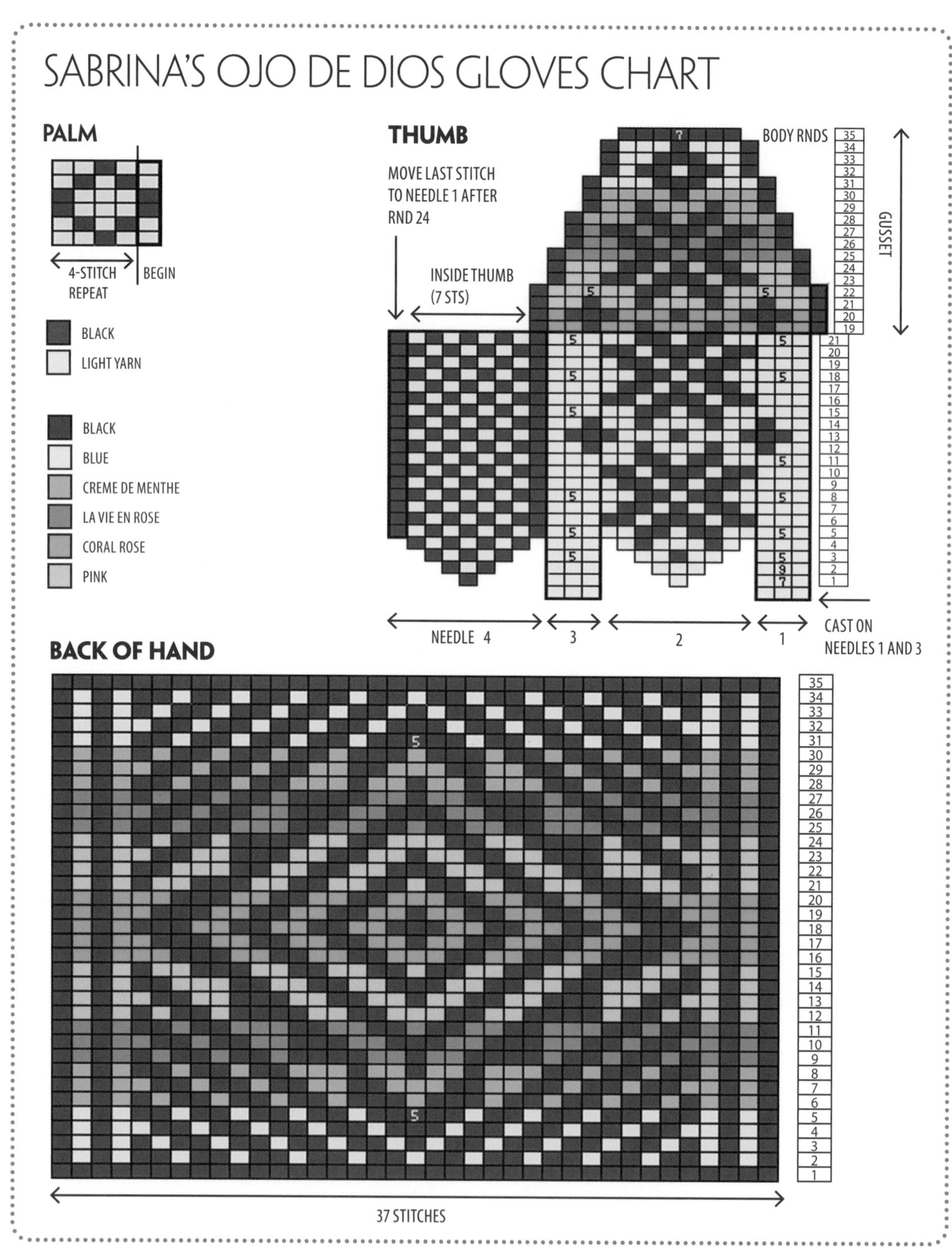

SHIRLEY'S SNOW HEART GLOVES

YARN

5 skeins of fingering weight yarn (approx 231yds [211m] per 1.76oz [50g]) in 5 different colors: Cranberry (MC), Chagrin, Violet, Sapphire and White House

The project shown was made using Lorna's Laces Shepherd Sock Solid (wool/nylon, 3.5oz/100g, 435yds/398m) in Cranberry and Chagrin, Expertly Dyed: Art by Science 100% Superwash Merino Fingering (100% merino, 1.76oz/50g, 220yds/201m) in Violet and Sapphire, and The Alpaca Yarn Company Glimmer (alpaca/polyester, 1.76oz/50g, 183yds/167m) in White House.

SHIRLEY'S SNOW HEART GLOVES CHART

FINGER

CRANBERRY
CHAGRIN
VIOLET
SAPPHIRE
WHITE HOUSE

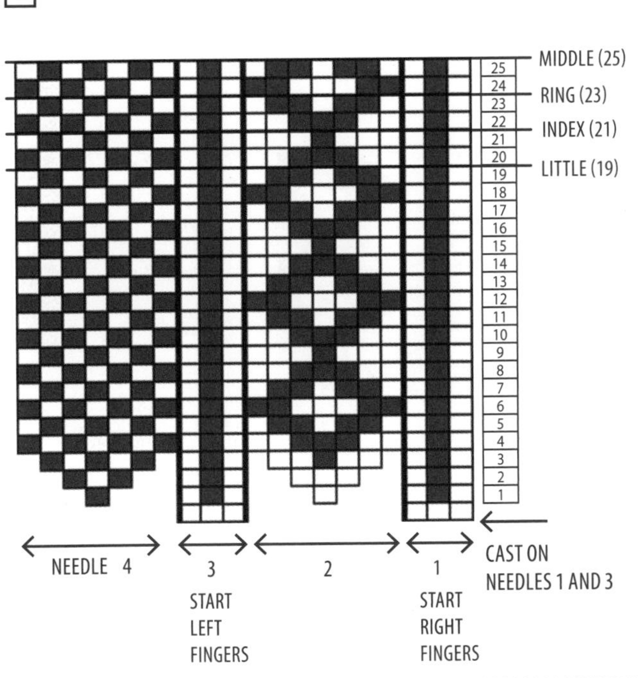

CORRUGATED RIBBING PATTERN

Rnds 1–4: K2 White House, p2 Sapphire.

Rnds 5–6: K2 White House, p2 Violet.

Rnds 7–8: K2 White House, p2 Cranberry.

Rnds 9–12: K2 White House, p2 Chagrin.

Rnds 13–14: K2 White House, p2 Cranberry.

Rnds 15–16: K2 White House, p2 Violet.

Rnds 17–20: K2 White House, p2 Sapphire.

GLOVE CONSTRUCTION

Note: For each glove, the palm contains the 28 sts from the palm side of the Fingers. The back-of-hand side contains the 28 sts from the fronts of the Fingers as well as the 3 edge sts each from the Little Finger and the Index Finger (34 sts)—62 sts.

Rnd 1: Knit this rnd with White House and slip the second stitch from each edge to maintain the vertical stripe and Increase 3 sts on the back-of-hand side—37 back-of-hand side sts and 28 palm-side sts—65 sts.

Rnds 2–35: Follow the general directions for gloves as well as the Palm, Thumb and Back-of-Hand Charts for Shirley's Snow Heart Gloves.

CUFF

Work 20 rnds using the Corrugated Ribbing Pattern. On the first rnd of ribbing, decrease 3 sts evenly on the snow heart side and 2 sts evenly on the palm side—60 sts. Bind off with White House.

SHIRLEY'S SNOW HEART GLOVES

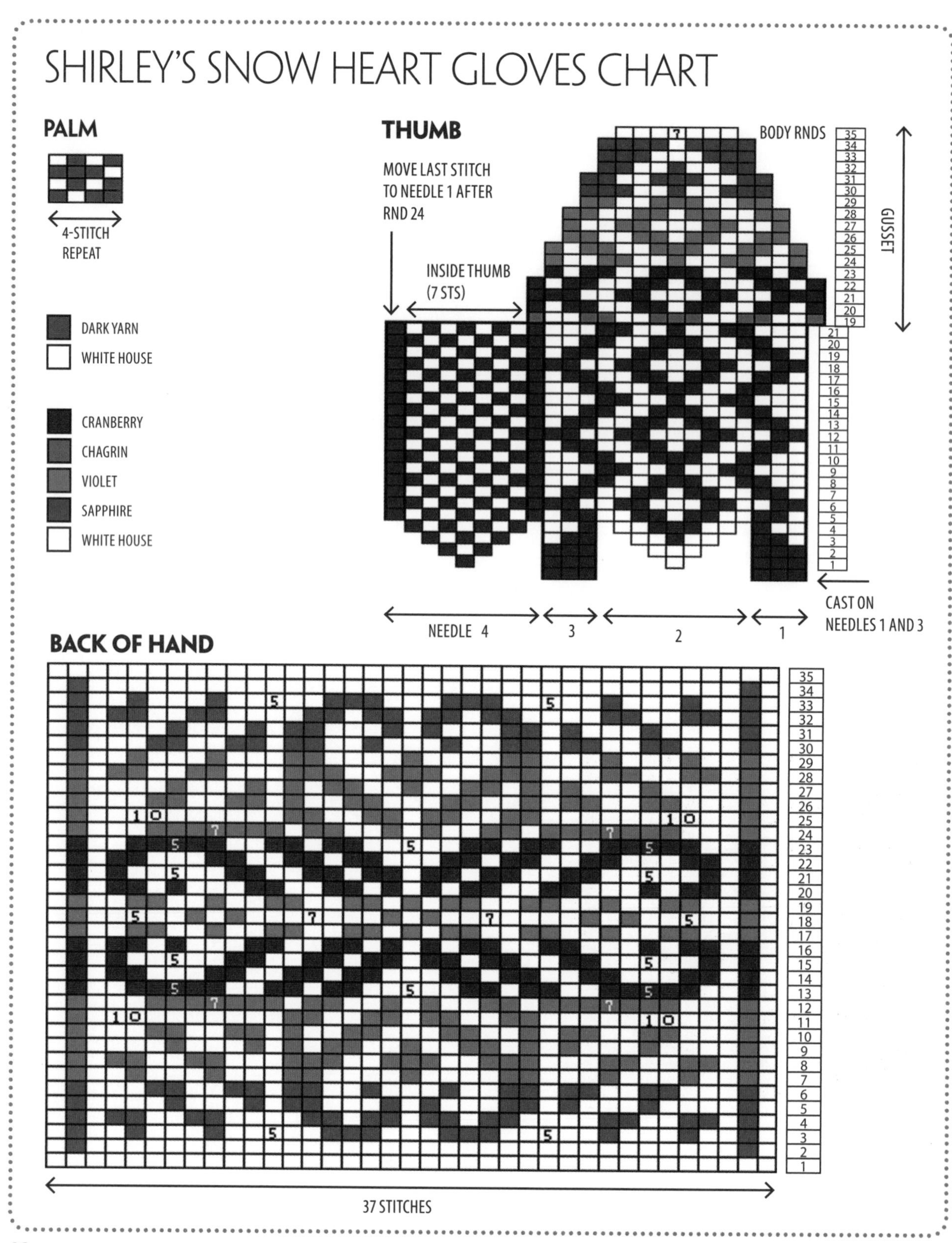

SHIRLEY'S SNOW HEART GLOVES CHART
PALM
4-STITCH REPEAT
DARK YARN
WHITE HOUSE
CRANBERRY
CHAGRIN
VIOLET
SAPPHIRE
WHITE HOUSE
THUMB
MOVE LAST STITCH TO NEEDLE 1 AFTER RND 24
INSIDE THUMB (7 STS)
BODY RNDS
GUSSET
CAST ON NEEDLES 1 AND 3
NEEDLE 4
3
2
1
BACK OF HAND
37 STITCHES

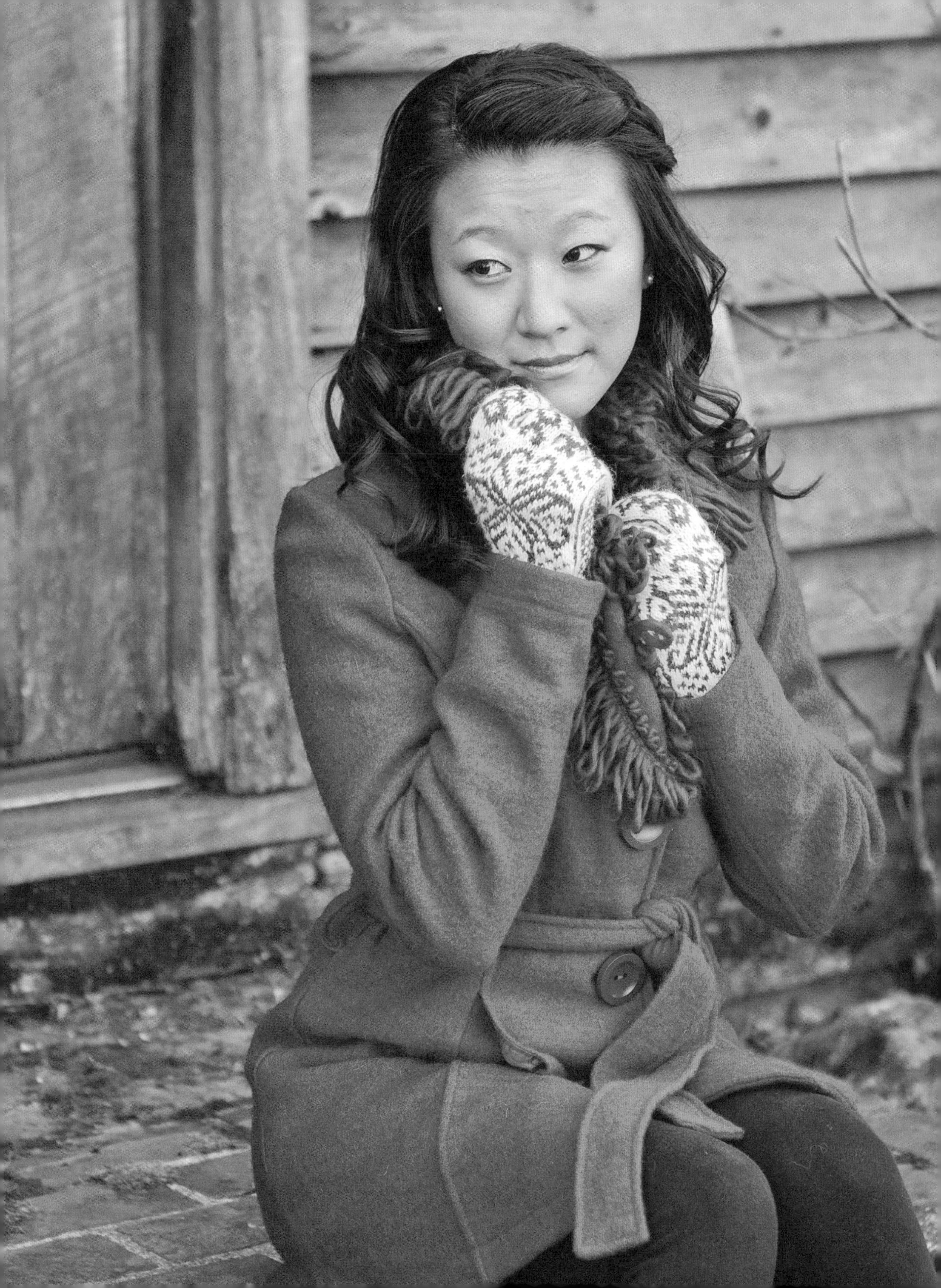

CHAPTER THREE

SOCKS, KNEE-HIGHS AND LEG WARMERS

MIDCALF SOCKS

Socks have long been my favorite "take-along" projects. I knit socks in the car, on the plane, at meetings and while waiting for appointments. I've knit socks for my parents, husband, siblings and daughter. Therefore, in a "Pride goeth before the fall" moment, I thought colorwork sock design would be a cake walk. Little did I realize that colorwork socks require about 30 percent more stitches than simple cable socks! I also learned much about sock anatomy while designing these socks, which I share below as lessons on how to modify or customize the designs to fit any foot.

ADJUSTING THE SIZE

Circumference: Adding one salt-and-pepper stitch to each side of the leg border adds about 1/2" (1cm) to the sock circumference. Adding two stitches to each side of each border adds eight stitches and increases the circumference by about 1" (2.5cm). You can also add gussets to the midcalf socks if they're too tight. Use the knee-high sock gussets as your guide.

Leg Length: To reduce the midcalf sock length, knit fewer rounds of ribbing. To increase the midcalf sock length, add a border similar to the one used in the knee-high patterns.

Ankle: The striped foot gusset controls the ease required to pull the sock over the ankle. Adding more stitches to the striped gussets provides more ease. Reducing the stitches tightens the sock at the ankle.

Foot Length: To lengthen the socks, add rounds to the sock border or add additional non-decrease rounds in the salt-and-pepper toe.

To shorten the length, remove rounds from the toe border or remove the non-decrease rounds that begin the salt-and-pepper toe.

SIZE

One size fits most women

MEASUREMENTS

Circumference: 8 1/4" (21cm)

Leg length: 9 1/2" (24cm)

Sock foot length: 9" (23cm)

NEEDLES

One set US 0 (2mm) double-pointed needles

If necessary, change needle size to obtain gauge.

NOTIONS

Stitch markers

Tapestry needle

GAUGE

4" (10cm) = 36 sts and 36 rnds in salt-and-pepper pattern

MIDCALF SOCKS

PATTERNS

HEEL PATTERN

Row 1 (RS): Sl 1, *k1 MC, k1 CC. Repeat from * across the row.

Row 2 (WS): Sl 1, *p1 CC, p1 MC. Repeat * across the row.

GUSSET STRIPE PATTERN

Row/Rnd 1: *K1 MC, k1 CC. Repeat from * to last stitch, k1 MC.

SALT-AND-PEPPER PATTERN

Row/Rnd 1: *K1 MC, k1 CC. Repeat from * around.

Row/Rnd 2: *K1 CC, k1 MC. Repeat from * around.

SOCKS

Cast on 80 sts onto 3 needles.

CUFF

Work 15 rnds of Corrugated Ribbing Pattern as indicted by your chosen design.

LEG

Knit Rnd 1 of the Pattern Chart in the designated color for all sts. Increase 4 sts on this first rnd—84 sts.

Knit each rnd beginning with Rnd 2 by knitting the Pattern Chart followed by the Leg Border Chart. Repeat twice for each rnd.

Work 2 repeats of the indicated rnds for the Pattern Chart while continuing the Leg Border Chart.

HEEL

Divide the sts for the Heel as indicated by your chosen design—43 Heel sts.

Using the sock colors indicated for your pattern, work 28 rows of the Heel Pattern.

TURN THE HEEL

Note: All decrease rows are worked in the established Heel Pattern.

Row 1: K27, k3tog tbl, k1, turn.

Row 2: P13, p3tog, p1, turn.

Row 3: K14, k3tog tbl, k1, turn.

Row 4: P15, p3tog, p1, turn.

Repeat the last 2 rows, adding 1 more stitch to each row until all of the Heel sts have been used—23 remaining Heel sts.

FOOT

Break off the Heel yarn. Begin knitting each rnd with the Foot Border and Pattern Charts. This avoids the jag that occurs when splitting the sole sts.

Needle 1 (Sock Main Pattern and Foot Borders): Knit the Foot Border Chart as indicated for your chosen design, then the Pattern Chart sts, followed by the Foot Border Chart—41 sts on Needle 1.

Needle 2 (Gusset and First Half of Sole Pattern): With a new needle, Needle 2, pick up and knit 9 sts along the Heel edge in the Gusset Stripe Pattern, pm. Pick up and knit 8 sts using the Sole Chart, knit the remaining 12 sts in the Sole Chart—29 sts on Needle 2 (9 gusset stripe sts and 20 sole sts).

Needle 3 (Second Half of Sole and Gusset): Knit 11 remaining Heel sts, continuing with the Sole Chart. Pick up and knit 8 sts along the Heel edge, continuing with the Sole Pattern, pm. Pick up and knit 9 sts using the Gusset Stripe Pattern—28 sts on Needle 3 (9 gusset stripe sts and 19 sole sts).

GUSSET RNDS

Rnd 1:

Needle 1: K41 following the Pattern and Foot Border Charts.

Needle 2: Follow the Gusset Stripe Pattern to marker, sm, work remaining sts in the Sole Chart.

Needle 3: Work in the Sole Chart to marker, sm, follow the Gusset Stripe Pattern for remaining sts.

Rnd 2:

Needle 1: Knit the Foot Border Chart, then the Pattern Chart, followed by the Foot Border Chart.

Needle 2: Sl 1,k1, psso in the Gusset Stripe Pattern. Follow the Gusset Stripe Pattern to marker, sm, work remaining sts in the Sole Chart to the end of the needle.

Needle 3: Work in the Sole Chart to marker, sm, work in the Gusset Stripe Pattern to the last 2 sts, k2tog.

Follow the gusset rnds until 1 st remains for each Gusset Stripe Pattern. Remove markers, but continue to knit the first stitch on Needle 2 and the last stitch on Needle 3 in the established color. Knit the remaining sole sts using the Sole Chart—41 sts on Needle 1, 21 sts on Needle 2 and 20 sts on Needle 3—82 sts (41 sole sts and 41 pattern sts).

TOE BORDER

Work the Toe Border Chart across Needle 1 while continuing to work the Sole Chart sts across Needles 2 and 3.

SHAPE THE TOE

Knit 1 rnd in MC. Knit 1 rnd in the Salt-and-Pepper Pattern while decreasing 9 sts evenly on Needle 1, 5 sts evenly on Needle 2 and 4 sts evenly on Needle 3—64 sts. Work Rnds 1–2 of the Toe decreases 4 times, then work Rnd 2 until 20 sts remain—10 sts on Needle 1, 5 sts on Needle 2 and 5 sts on Needle 3.

Note: The Toe uses a double decrease to keep the established Salt-and-Pepper Pattern.

Rnd 1: Work in the Salt-and-Pepper Pattern.

Rnd 2:

Needle 1: Slip last st on Needle 3 onto Needle 1, k3tog, knit in the Salt-and-Pepper Pattern to the last stitch.

Needle 2: Slip last st from Needle 1 onto Needle 2, k3tog, knit the remaining sts using the Salt-and-Pepper Pattern.

Needle 3: Knit in the Salt-and-Pepper Pattern.

FINISHING

Place the 5 sts from Needle 2 and the 5 sts from Needle 3 on one needle. You now have 10 sts on each of 2 needles. With MC, Kitchener stitch the Toe closed.

CONVERSION TO KNEE-HIGH SOCKS

To convert any of the midcalf sock patterns to knee-high socks, follow these steps:

1. Follow the knee-high sock directions (see page 104).
2. Increase the ribbing to 20 rnds. If there is a matching glove or mitten design, use this as your model. If none exists, add 1 rnd to each end of the ribbing, 1 rnd in the middle and 2 rnds symmetrically somewhere in between.
3. Add leg gussets to the leg border. If the first and last stitch of the pattern uses MC yarn, use the Leg Gusset Chart from *Laurie's Chrysanthemum Knee-Highs* (see page 112) as your model. If the first and last stitch of the design is in the light yarn, use the Leg Gusset Chart from *Lisa's Double Star Knee-Highs* (see page 108) as your model.
4. Add a knee border. Knit this using the Sole Chart.

KATEY'S ACORN SOCKS

YARN

7 skeins of fingering weight yarn (approx 231yds [211m] per 1.76oz [50g]) in 7 different colors: Bark, Fig, Vandyke Brown, Byzantine, Camel, Champagne and Natural

The project shown was made using Cascade Yarns Heritage 150 Solids (merino/nylon, 5.3oz/150g, 492yds/450m) in Bark, Madelinetosh Tosh Merino Light (100% merino wool, 3.5oz/100g, 420yds/384m) in Fig and Byzantine, Cascade Yarns Heritage Silk (merino/silk, 3.5oz/100g, 437yds/400m) in Camel and Vandyke Brown, Cherry Tree Hill/Louet Gems Fingering (100% merino, 1.76oz/50g, 185yds/169m) in Champagne and Valley Yarns Huntington (merino/nylon, 1.76oz/50g, 218yds/199m) in Natural.

CORRUGATED RIBBING PATTERN

Rounds 1-3: K2 Bark, p2 Camel.

Rounds 4-5: K2 Fig, p2 Camel.

Rounds 6-7: K2 Vandyke Brown, p2 Champagne.

Round 8: K2 Byzantine, p2 Natural.

Rounds 9-10: K2 Vandyke Brown, p2 Champagne.

Rounds 11-12: K2 Fig, p2 Camel.

Rounds 13-15: K2 Bark, p2 Camel.

SOCK CONSTRUCTION

CUFF

With Bark, cast on 80 sts onto 3 needles—28 sts on Needle 1, 24 sts on Needle 2 and 28 sts on Needle 3. Work 15 rnds of the Corrugated Ribbing Pattern.

LEG

Work Rnd 1 with Bark while increasing 4 sts evenly around—84 sts. Knit 2 repeats of Rnds 2–34 of the Pattern Chart with the Leg Border Chart.

HEEL

Note: For this section, Bark is MC and Camel is CC.

Place 4 sts from each border on the same needle as the 35 main pattern sts—43 sts. Knit the Heel Pattern.

FOOT

Knit the gusset stripes beginning with Bark (MC)/Camel (CC). Work Rnds 2-34 of the Pattern Chart coupled with the Foot Border Chart, the Sole Chart and the Gusset Stripe Pattern.

TOE BORDER

Knit 1 rnd with Byzantine across Needle 1 while continuing the Sole Chart across Needles 2 and 3.

Knit the Toe Border Chart across Needle 1 while continuing the Sole Chart across Needles 2 and 3.

Knit 1 rnd with Byzantine.

TOE

Knit the Toe with Byzantine (MC)/Natural (CC).

KATEY'S ACORN SOCKS CHART

TOE BORDER

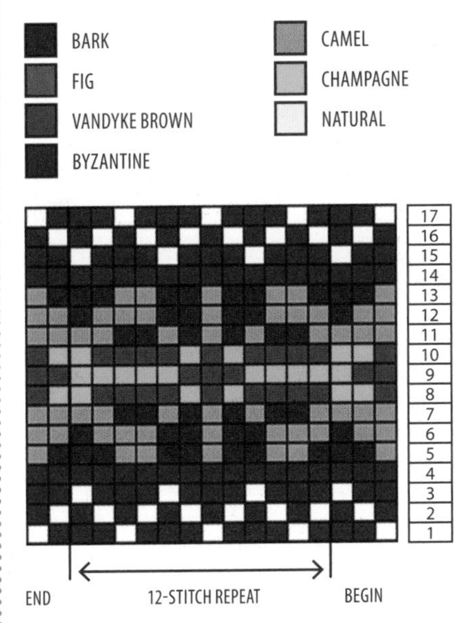

KATEY'S ACORN SOCKS

KATEY'S ACORN SOCKS CHART

LEG BORDER

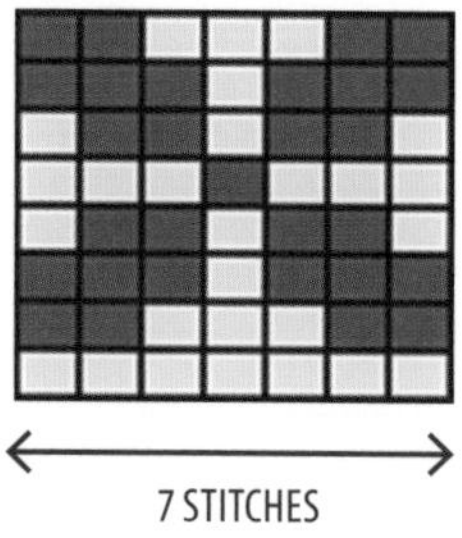

7 STITCHES

FOOT BORDER

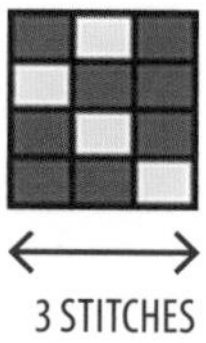

3 STITCHES

SOLE

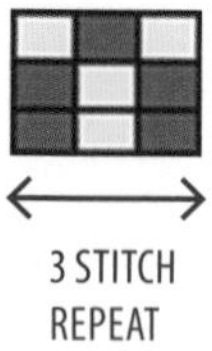

3 STITCH REPEAT

DARK YARN

LIGHT YARN

BARK

FIG

VANDYKE BROWN

BYZANTINE

CAMEL

CHAMPAGNE

NATURAL

PATTERN

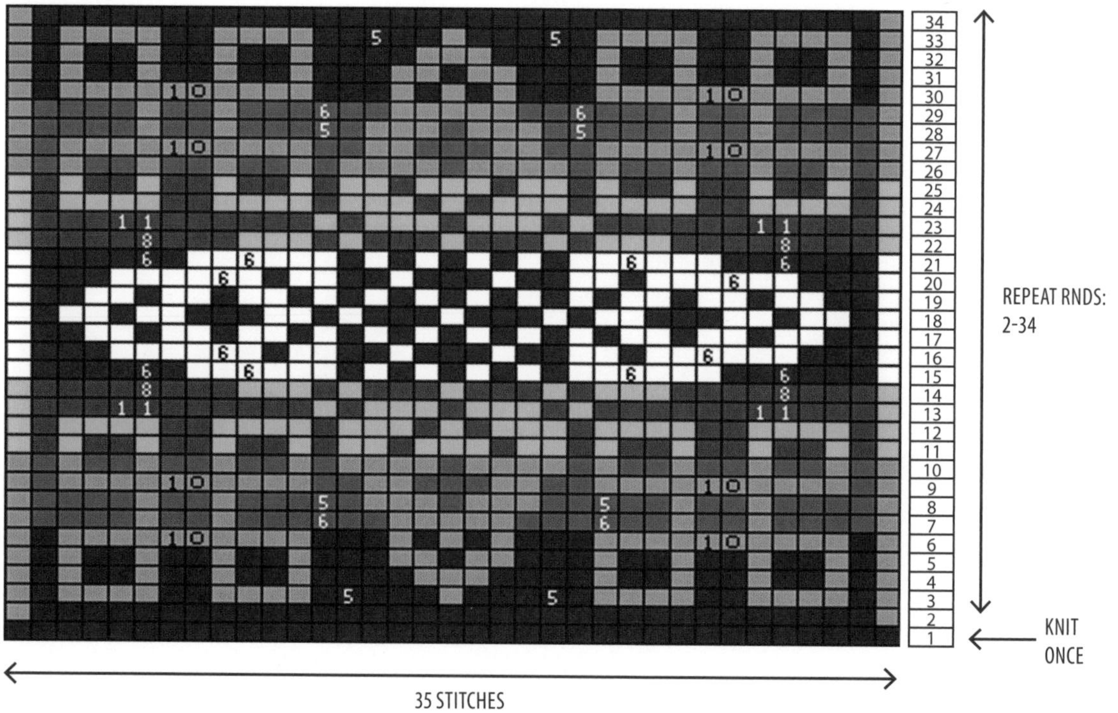

REPEAT RNDS: 2-34

KNIT ONCE

35 STITCHES

LYNDI'S FEATHERED STAR SOCKS

YARN

5 skeins of fingering weight yarn (approx 231yds [211m] per 1.76oz [50g]) in 5 different colors: Turquoise, Nebula, Forestry, Jade and Natural

The project shown was made using Cascade Yarns Heritage Silk (merino/silk, 3.5oz/100g, 437yds/400m) in Turquoise, Madelinetosh Tosh Merino Light (100% merino wool, 3.5oz/100g, 420yds/384m) in Nebula, Forestry and Jade, and Knit Picks Bare Stroll Fingering Sock (superwash merino/nylon, 3.5oz/100g, 462yds/422m) in Natural.

CORRUGATED RIBBING PATTERN

Rounds 1-3: K2 Nebula, p2 Natural.

Rounds 4-6: K2 Forestry, p2 Natural.

Rounds 7-9: K2 Jade, p2 Natural.

Rounds 10-12: K2 Forestry, p2 Natural.

Rounds 13-15: K2 Nebula, p2 Natural.

SOCK CONSTRUCTION

CUFF

With Nebula, cast 80 sts onto 3 needles—28 sts on Needle 1, 24 sts on Needle 2 and 28 sts on Needle 3. Work 15 rnds of the Corrugated Ribbing Pattern.

LEG

Work Rnd 1 in Turquoise while increasing 4 sts evenly around—84 sts. Knit 2 repeats of Rnds 2–35 of the Pattern Chart with the Leg Border Chart.

HEEL

Note: For this section, Jade is MC and Natural is CC.

Place 4 sts from each border on the same needle as the 35 main pattern sts—43 sts. Knit the Heel Pattern.

FOOT

Note: For this section, Turquoise is MC and Natural is CC.

Knit the Gusset Stripe Pattern beginning with Turquoise (MC)/Natural (CC). Work Rnds 2–35 of the Pattern Chart, coupled with the Foot Border Chart, the Sole Chart and the Gusset Stripe Pattern.

TOE BORDER

Knit 1 rnd with Nebula across Needle 1 while continuing the Sole Chart across Needles 2 and 3.

Knit the Toe Border Chart across Needle 1 while continuing the Sole Chart across Needles 2 and 3. Knit 1 rnd with Nebula.

TOE

Knit the Toe with Jade (MC)/Natural (CC).

LYNDI'S FEATHERED STAR SOCKS CHART

TOE BORDER

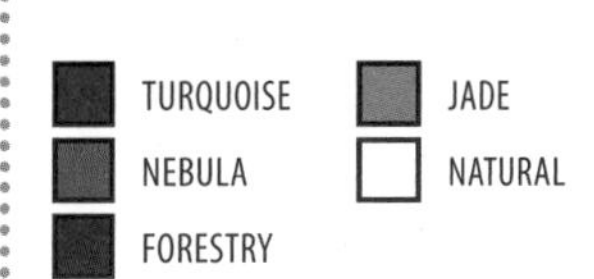

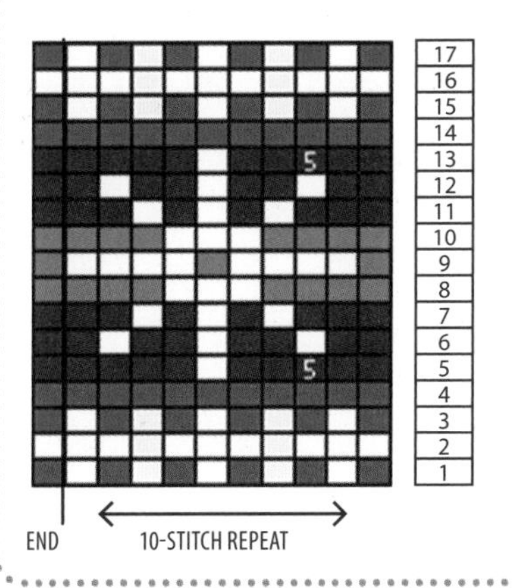

LYNDI'S FEATHERED STAR SOCKS

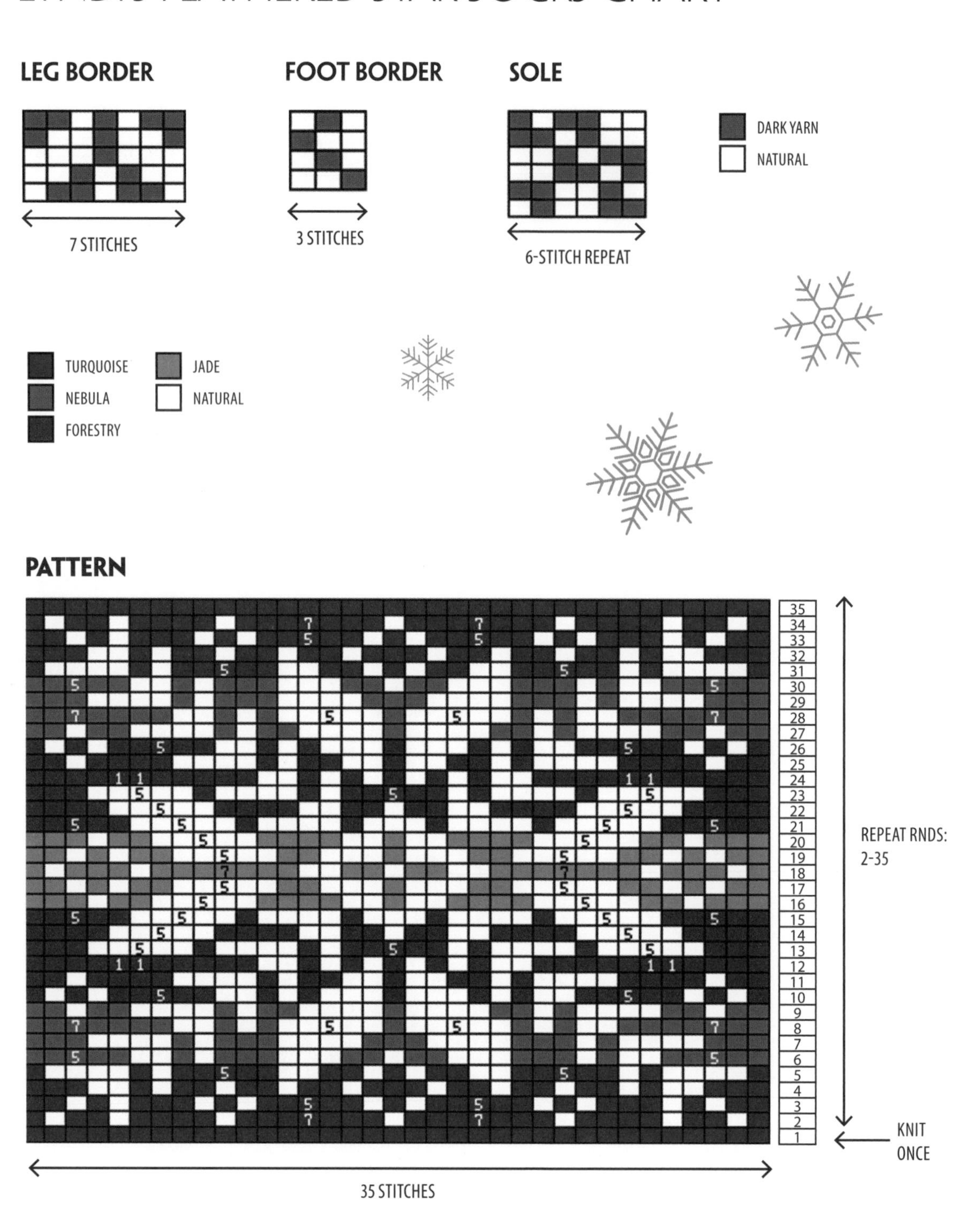

REATE THE LOOK
ndi's Nine-Point Allover
m pattern: **Page 30**

LYNDI'S FEATHERED STAR SOCKS

ALTERNATE COLORWAY

YARN

5 skeins of fingering weight yarn (approx 231yds [211m] per 1.76oz [50g]) in 5 different colors: Dark Sunset, Mauve, Trodden, Flour Sack and Champagne

This alternate colorway was made using Cascade Yarns Heritage Paints (merino/nylon, 3.5oz/100g, 437yds/400m) in Dark Sunset, Araucania Ranco Solid (wool/nylon, 3.5oz/100g, 376yds/344m) in Mauve, Madelinetosh Tosh Merino Light (100% merino wool, 3.5oz/100g, 420yds/384m) in Trodden, Madelinetosh Tosh Sock (100% merino wool, 4oz/114g, 395yds/361m) in Flour Sack and Cherry Tree Hill Louet Gems Fingering (100% merino, 1.76oz/50g, 185yds/169m) in Champagne.

SOCK CONSTRUCTION

CUFF

With Dark Sunset, cast 80 sts onto 3 needles—28 sts on Needle 1, 24 sts on Needle 2 and 28 sts on Needle 3. Work 15 rnds of the Corrugated Ribbing Pattern.

LEG

Work Rnd 1 in Dark Sunset while increasing 4 sts evenly around—84 sts. Knit 2 repeats of Rnds 2–35 of the Pattern Chart with the Leg Border Chart.

HEEL

Note: For this section, Dark Sunset is MC and Flour Sack is CC.

Place 4 sts from each border on the same needle as the 35 main pattern sts—43 sts. Knit the Heel Pattern.

FOOT

Note: For this section, Dark Sunset is MC and Flour Sack is CC.

Knit the Gusset Stripe Pattern beginning with Dark Sunset (MC)/Flour Sack (CC). Work Rnds 2–35 of the Pattern Chart, coupled with the Foot Border Chart, the Sole Chart and the Gusset Stripe Pattern.

TOE BORDER

Knit 1 rnd with Flour Sack across Needle 1 while continuing the Sole Chart across Needles 2 and 3.

Knit the Toe Border Chart across Needle 1 while continuing the Sole Chart across Needles 2 and 3. Knit 1 rnd with Flour Sack.

TOE

Knit the Toe with Dark Sunset (MC)/Flour Sack (CC).

CORRUGATED RIBBING PATTERN

Rnds 1–3: K2 Dark Sunset, p2 Trodden.

Rnds 4–6: K2 Dark Sunset, p2 Champagne.

Rnds 7–9: K2 Dark Sunset, p2 Flour Sack.

Rnds 10–12: K2 Dark Sunset, p2 Champagne.

Rnds 13–15: K2 Dark Sunset, p2 Trodden.

LYNDI'S FEATHERED STAR SOCKS CHART

ALTERNATE - TOE BORDER

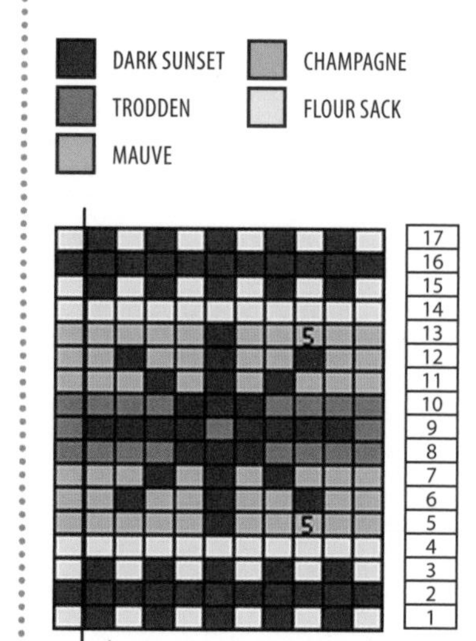

LYNDI'S FEATHERED STAR SOCKS CHART

ALTERNATE COLORWAY

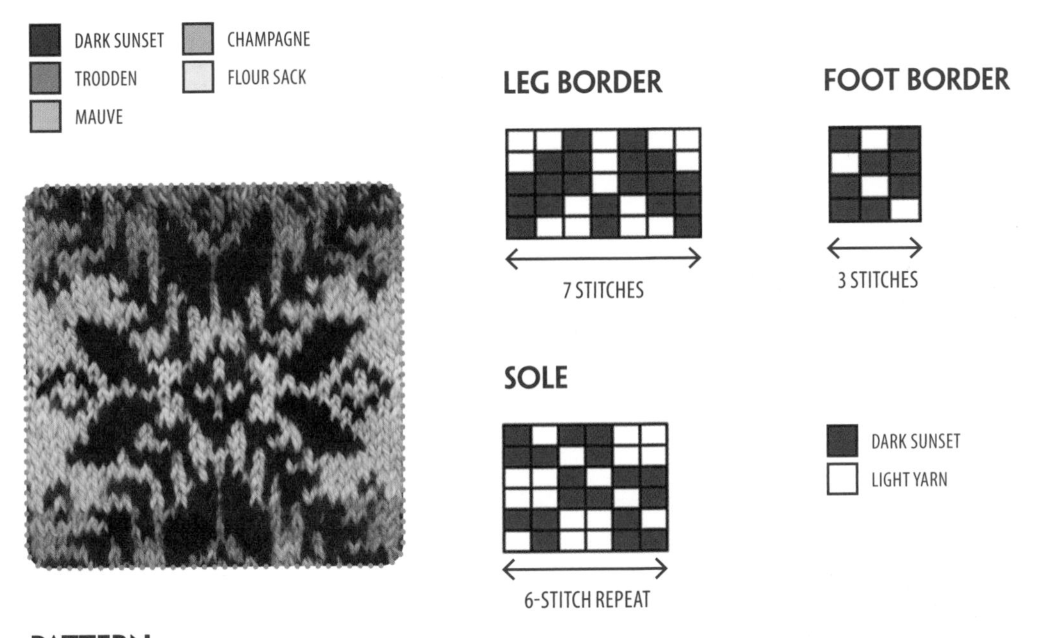

PATTERN

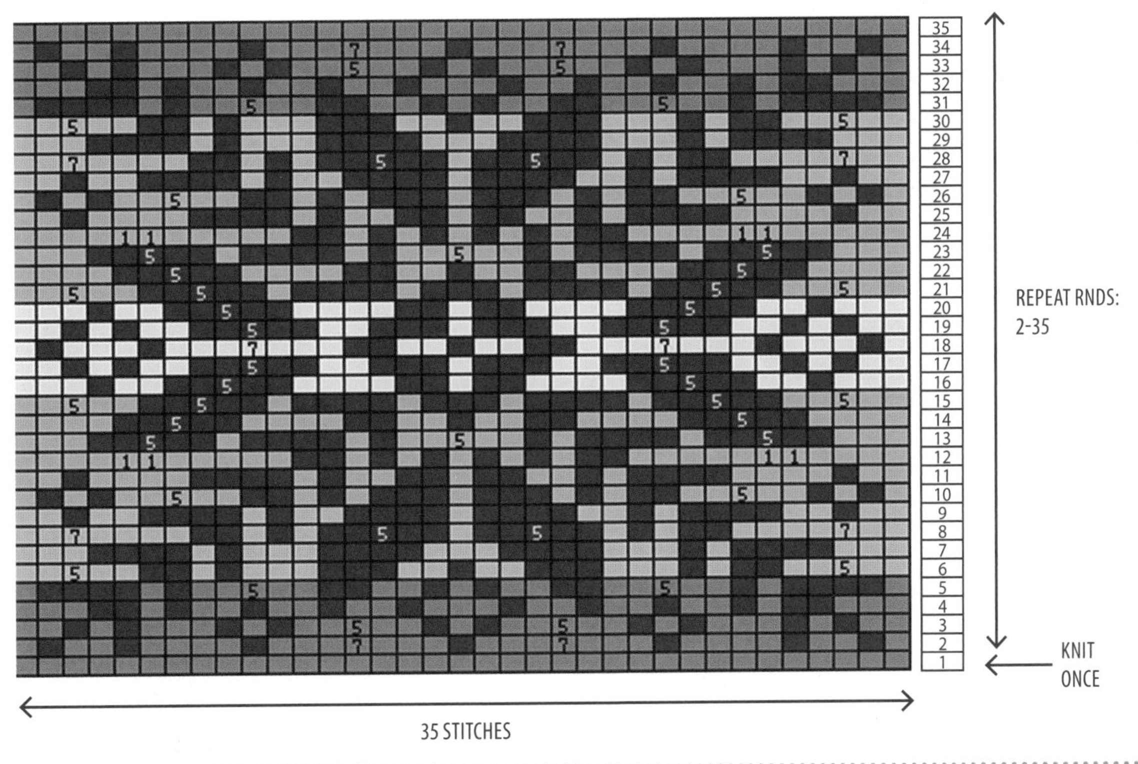

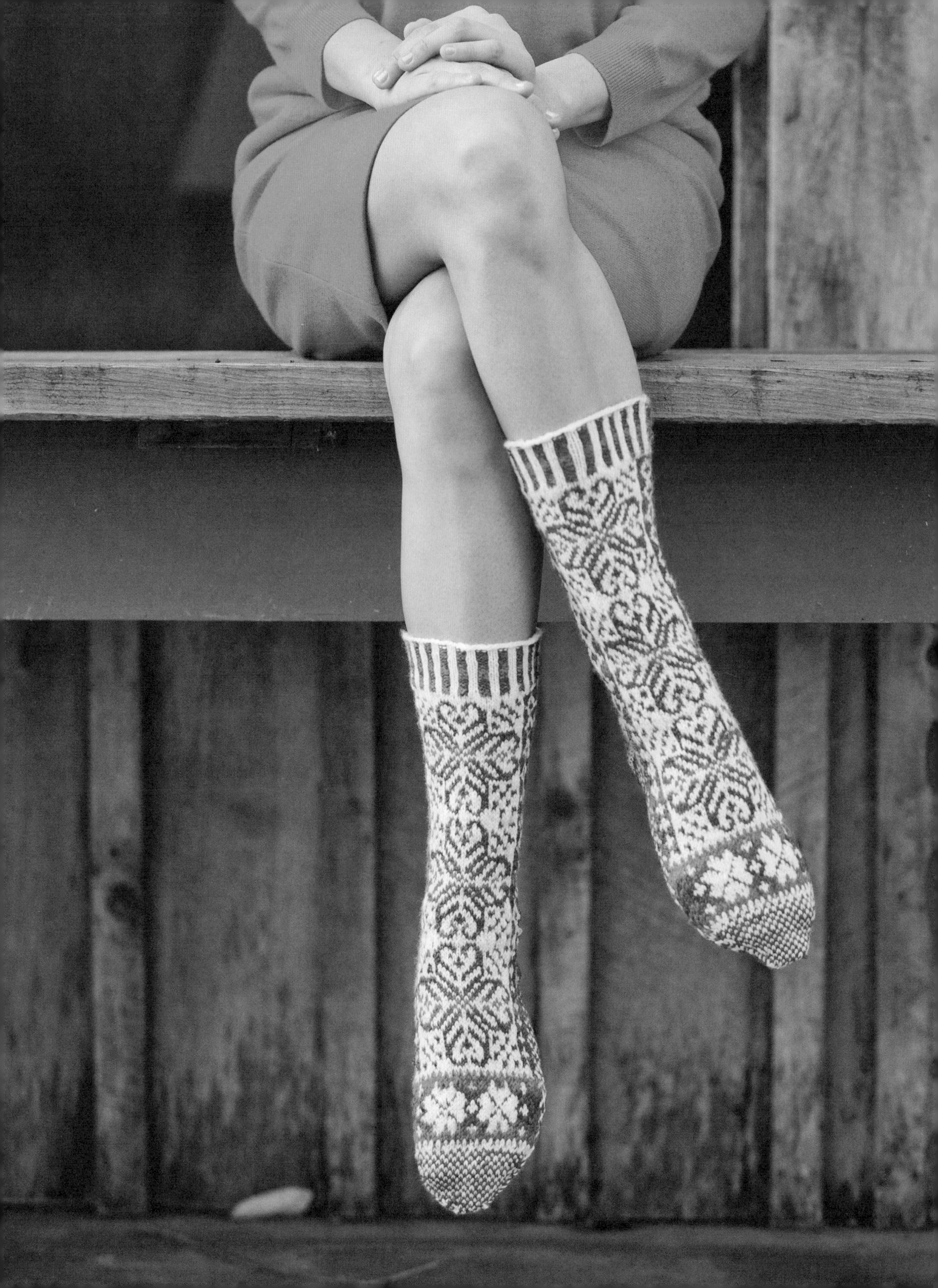

SHIRLEY'S SNOW HEART SOCKS

YARN

5 skeins of fingering weight yarn (approx 231yds [211m] per 1.76oz [50g]) in 5 different colors: Violet, Sapphire, Cranberry, Chagrin and Natural

The project shown was made using Expertly Dyed: Art by Science 100% Superwash Merino Fingering (100% merino, 1.76oz/50g, 220yds/201m) in Violet and Sapphire, Lorna's Laces Shepherd Sock Solid (wool/nylon, 3.5oz/100g, 435yds/398m) in Cranberry and Chagrin, and Knit Picks Bare Stroll Fingering Sock (superwash merino/nylon, 3.5oz/100g, 462yds/422m) in Natural.

CORRUGATED RIBBING PATTERN

Rnds 1–3: K2 Natural, p2 Sapphire.

Rnds 4–6: K2 Natural, p2 Violet.

Rnds 7–9: K2 Natural, p2 Chagrin.

Rnds 10–12: K2 Natural, p2 Violet.

Rnds 13–15: K2 Natural, p2 Sapphire.

SOCK CONSTRUCTION

CUFF

With Natural, cast on 80 sts onto 3 needles—28 sts on Needle 1, 24 sts on Needle 2 and 28 sts on Needle 3. Work 15 rnds of the Corrugated Ribbing Pattern.

LEG

Work Rnd 1 with Natural while increasing 4 sts evenly around—84 sts. Work Rnd 2 border as k7 Sapphire. Knit Rnds 3–33 of the Pattern Chart with the Leg Border Chart. Knit Rnds 2–33 of the Pattern Chart with the Leg Border Chart.

HEEL

Note: For this section, Natural is MC and Cranberry is CC.

Place 4 sts from each border on the same needle as the 35 Sock Chart sts—43 sts. Knit the Heel Pattern.

FOOT

Note: For this section, Sapphire is MC and Natural is CC.

Knit the gusset stripes beginning with Sapphire (MC)/White (CC). Work Rnds 2–33 of the Pattern Chart, coupled with the Foot Border Chart, the Sole Chart and the Gusset Stripe Pattern.

TOE BORDER

Knit 1 rnd with Natural across Needle 1 while continuing the Sole Chart across Needles 2 and 3. Knit the Toe Border Chart across Needle 1 while continuing the Sole Chart across Needles 2 and 3.

TOE

Knit the Toe with Natural (MC)/Cranberry (CC).

SHIRLEY'S SNOW HEART SOCKS CHART

TOE BORDER

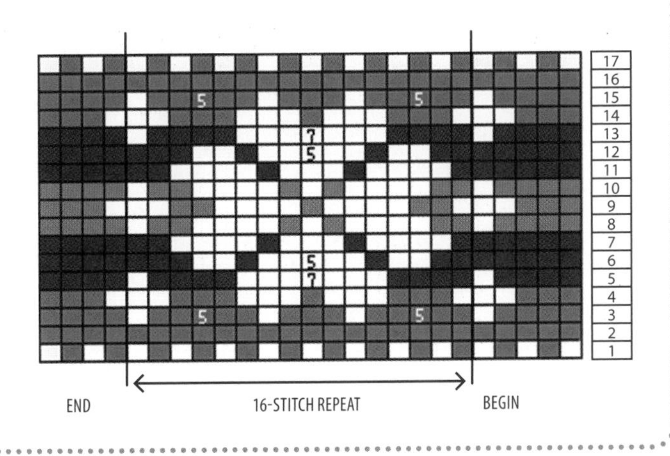

SHIRLEY'S SNOW HEART SOCKS

SHIRLEY'S SNOW HEART SOCKS CHART

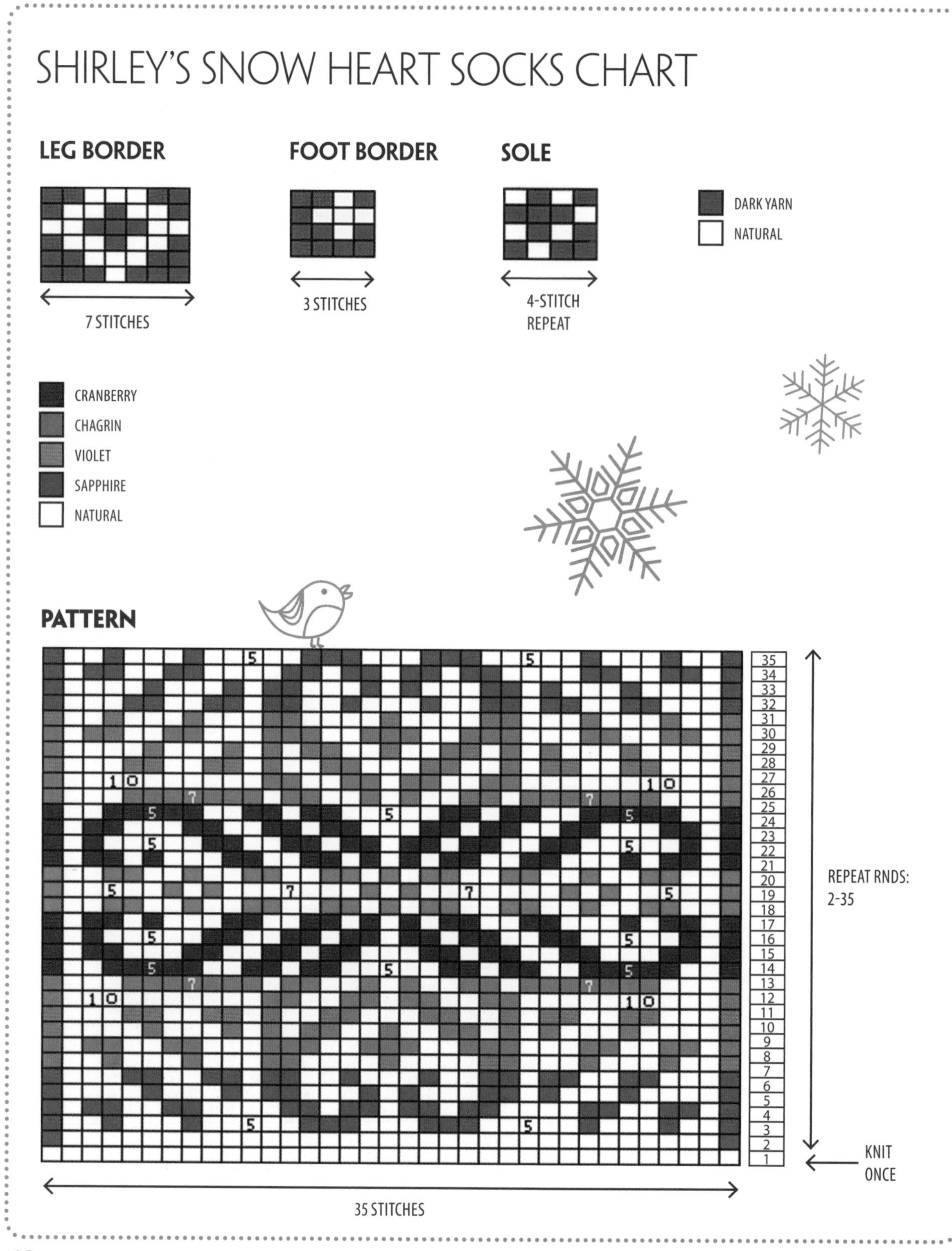

KNEE-HIGHS

SIZE

One size fits most women

MEASUREMENTS

Circumference: 8 1/4" (21cm)

Leg Length: 18" (45.5cm)

Foot Length: 9" (23cm)

NEEDLES

One 6" (15cm) set of US 0 double-pointed needles

One 8" (20.5cm) set of US 0 (2mm) double-pointed needles

If necessary, change needle size to obtain correct gauge.

NOTIONS

Stitch markers

Tapestry needle

GAUGE

4" (10cm) = 36 sts and 36 rnds in salt-and-pepper pattern

PATTERNS

HEEL PATTERN

Row 1 (RS): Sl 1, *k1 MC, k1 CC. Repeat from * across the row.

Row 2 (WS): Sl 1, *p1 CC, p1 MC. Repeat from * across the row.

GUSSET STRIPE PATTERN

Row/Rnd 1: *K1 MC, k1 CC. Repeat from * to last stitch, k1 MC.

SALT-AND-PEPPER PATTERN

Row/Rnd 1: *K1 MC, k1 CC. Repeat from * around.
Row/Rnd 2: *K1 CC, k1 MC. Repeat from * around.

When I was a child, girls could only wear skirts or jumpers to school. Knee-high socks were our "leg savers," especially in cold Green Bay, Wisconsin. Choosing knee-highs that fit correctly was a risky task since store etiquette did not allow us to try on these socks before purchasing them. Knee-highs that were too tight left red ridges at the knees, while knee-highs that were too loose sunk helplessly to our ankles. When I designed the knee-highs for this book, I remembered my childhood. I wanted knee-highs that were snug enough to stay up, but not so snug that they cut off circulation.

ADJUSTING THE SIZE

Most women have a much wider calf than ankle. You can design socks that reflect this difference through changes in needle size. My first unsuccessful attempt at knee highs used this technique. Not only did the changes in pattern size look awful, the socks were still too tight at the calf. I prefer adding salt-and-pepper gussets to the vertical bands that separate the main motifs. This produces the correct tapering, and the knitter can adjust the gusset width easily. If you need a wider sock, add salt-and-pepper stitches to each side of the gusset. Each addition increases the gusset by two stitches and the sock by four stitches—about 1/2" (1cm). If you need a narrower gusset, reduce the number of salt-and-pepper stitches.

For other tips on adjusting the size, see the Socks section on page 86.

KNEE-HIGH SOCKS

CUFF

With MC, cast on 96 sts. Knit the Corrugated Ribbing Pattern indicated by your chosen design.

KNEE BORDER

Knit the Knee Border as indicated by your chosen design.

LEG

Knit 1 rnd with MC. Knit pattern Rnd 1 with MC as follows: *Knit in the Pattern Chart to the last stitch of the Pattern Chart, pm, knit the last stitch, work the Knee-High Gusset Chart, work the Leg Border Chart, work the Knee-High Gusset Chart, knit the first stitch of the Pattern Chart, pm. Repeat from * once.

Knit repeat rnds as indicated by your design while knitting the Leg Border and Knee-High Gusset Charts.

Knit gusset decrease rnd as indicated every sixteenth rnd twice, every eighth rnd twice, then every fourth rnd once. Continue following the Pattern Chart and Leg Border Chart only.

Knee-High Gusset Decrease Rnd: Knit in the Pattern Chart to marker, sm, sl 1, k1, psso, work in the Knee-High Gusset and Leg Border Charts as established to the last 2 sts before marker, k2tog, sm, knit in the Sock Chart to marker, sm, sl 1, k1, psso, work in the Knee-High Gusset and Leg Border Charts as established to the last st before marker. Move last stitch to Needle 1, k2tog at beginning of next rnd.

HEEL

Divide the sts for the Heel as indicated by your design—43 sts.

Using the colors indicated for your design, work the 28 rows of the Heel Pattern.

TURN THE HEEL

Note: All decrease rows are worked in the established Heel Pattern.

Row 1: K27, k3tog tbl, k1, turn.

Row 2: P13, p3tog, p1, turn.

Row 3: K14, k3tog tbl, k1, turn.

Row 4: P15, p3tog, p1, turn.

Repeat the last 2 rows, adding 1 more stitch to each row, until all of the Heel sts have been used—23 remaining Heel sts.

FOOT

Break off the Heel yarn. Begin knitting each rnd with the Foot Border and Pattern Charts. This avoids the jag that occurs when splitting the sole sts.

Needle 1 (Sock Chart and Foot Borders): Knit the Foot Border Chart as indicated for your pattern, then the Pattern Chart, followed by the Foot Border—41 sts on Needle 1.

Needle 2 (Gusset and First Half of Sole Chart): With a new needle, pick up and knit 9 sts along the Heel edge in the Gusset Stripe Pattern, pm. Pick up and knit 8 sts using the Sole Chart, knit the remaining 12 sts continuing with the Sole Chart—29 sts on Needle 2 (9 gusset stripe sts and 20 sole sts).

Needle 3 (Second Half of Sole and Gusset): Knit 11 remaining Heel sts continuing with the Sole Chart. Pick up and knit 8 sts along the Heel edge continuing with the Sole Chart, pm. Pick up and knit 9 sts using the Gusset Stripe Pattern—28 sts on Needle 3 (9 gusset stripe sts and 19 sole sts).

GUSSET ROUNDS

Rnd 1:

Needle 1: K41 sts following the Pattern and Foot Border Charts.

Needle 2: Follow the Gusset Stripe Pattern to marker, sm, work the Sole Chart for rem sts.

Needle 3: Continue in the Sole Chart to marker, sm, following the Gusset Stripe Pattern for remaining sts.

Rnd 2:

Needle 1: Knit the Foot Border Chart, then the Sock Chart, followed by the Foot Border Chart.

Needle 2: Sl 1, k1, psso in the Gusset Stripe Pattern. Work the Gusset Stripe Pattern to marker, sm, work the Sole Chart to the end of the needle.

Needle 3: Continue in the Sole Chart to marker, sm, work the Gusset Stripe Pattern to last 2 sts, k2tog.

Follow the gusset rnds until 1 st remains for each Gusset Stripe Pattern. Remove markers, but continue to knit the first stitch on Needle 2 and the last stitch on Needle 3 in the established color. Knit the remaining sole sts using the Sole Chart—41 sts on Needle 1, 21 sts on Needle 2 and 20 sts on Needle 3—82 sts (41 sole sts and 41 pattern sts).

TOE BORDER

Work the Toe Border Chart across Needle 1 while continuing to work the Sole Chart across Needles 2 and 3.

SHAPE THE TOE

Knit 1 rnd in MC. Knit 1 rnd in the Salt-and-Pepper Pattern while decreasing 9 sts on Needle 1, 5 sts on Needle 2 and 4 sts on Needle 3—64 sts. Work Rnds 1 and 2 of the toe decreases 4 times, then work Rnd 2 only until 20 sts remain—10 sts on Needle 1, 5 sts on Needle 2 and 5 sts on Needle 3.

Note: The Toe uses a double decrease to keep the established Salt-and-Pepper Pattern.

Rnd 1: Work in the Salt-and-Pepper Pattern.

Rnd 2:

Needle 1: Slip the last stitch on Needle 3 onto Needle 1, k3tog, knit in the Salt-and-Pepper Pattern to the last stitch.

Needle 2: Slip the last stitch from Needle 1 onto Needle 2, k3tog, knit the remaining sts in the Salt-and-Pepper Pattern.

Needle 3: Knit in the Salt-and-Pepper Pattern.

FINISHING

Place the 5 sts from Needle 2 and the 5 sts from Needle 3 on one needle. You now have 10 sts on each of 2 needles. With MC, Kitchener stitch the Toe closed.

CONVERSION TO MID-CALF SOCKS

To convert any of the knee-high sock patterns to midcalf socks, follow these steps:

1. Follow the midcalf sock directions (see page 86).

2. Use only 15 rnds of ribbing. Do this by removing 1 rnd from each end of the ribbing, 1 rnd in the middle and 2 rnds symmetrically from somewhere in between.

3. Omit the leg gussets; knit only the leg border.

4. Omit the knee border.

LISA'S DOUBLE STAR KNEE-HIGHS

YARN

7 skeins of fingering weight yarn (approx 231yds [211m] per 1.76oz [50g]) in 7 different colors: Black, Fig, Charcoal, Chestnut, Latte, Linen Grey and Natural

The project shown was made using Valley Yarns Huntington (merino/nylon, 1.76oz/50g, 218yds/199m) in Black and Natural, Madelinetosh Tosh Merino Light (100% merino wool, 3.5oz/100g, 420yds/384m) in Charcoal and Fig, Cherry Tree Hill/Louet Gems Fingering (100% merino, 1.76oz/50g, 185yds/169m) in Linen Grey and Araucania Itata Solid (wool/bamboo/silk, 3.5oz/100g, 430yds/393m) in Chestnut and Latte.

CORRUGATED RIBBING PATTERN

Rnds 1–4: K2 Black, p2 Linen Grey.

Rnds 5–6: K2 Charcoal, p2 Linen Grey.

Rnds 7–8: K2 Fig, p2 Latte.

Rnds 9–12: K2 Chestnut, p2 Natural.

Rnds 13–14: K2 Fig, p2 Latte.

Rnds 15–16: K2 Charcoal, p2 Linen Grey.

Rnds 17–20: K2 Black, p2 Linen Grey.

KNEE-HIGH CONSTRUCTION

Note: Unless otherwise indicated, Black is MC.

CUFF

With Black, cast on 96 sts. Knit 20 rnds of the Corrugated Ribbing Pattern.

KNEE BORDER

Knit 2 rnds with Black, increasing 8 sts on first rnd—104 sts. Knit 12 rnds of the Sole Chart as follows: Knit 4 rnds with Chestnut/Natural, knit 4 rnds with Fig/Latte, knit 4 rnds with Chestnut/Natural. Knit 2 rnds with Black.

LEG

Knit 3 repeats of Rnds 2–35 of the Pattern Chart while knitting the Leg Border and Knee-High Gusset Charts.

HEEL

Place 4 sts from each border on the same needle as the 35 Pattern Chart sts—43 sts. Knit the Heel Pattern with Fig (MC)/Latte (CC).

FOOT

Knit the Gusset Stripe Pattern beginning with Black (MC)/Linen Grey (CC). Work Rnds 2–35 of the Pattern Chart coupled with the Foot Border Chart, Sole Chart and Gusset Stripe Pattern.

TOE BORDER

Knit 1 rnd with Chestnut across Needle 1 while continuing the Sole Chart across Needles 2 and 3.

Knit the Toe Border Chart across Needle 1 while continuing the Sole Chart across Needles 2 and 3. Knit 1 rnd with Chestnut.

TOE

Knit the Toe with Fig (MC)/Latte (CC).

LISA'S DOUBLE STAR KNEE-HIGHS CHART

TOE BORDER

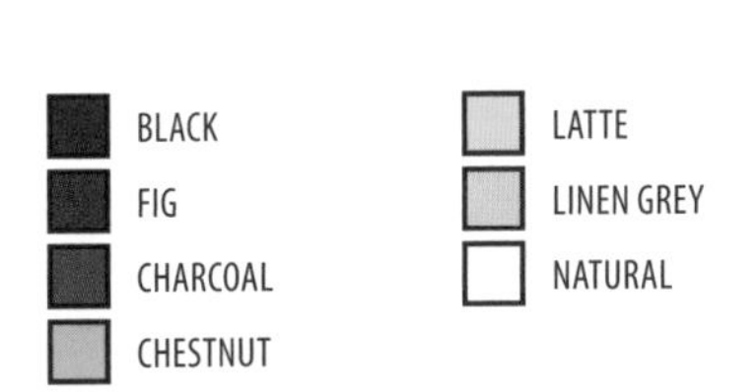

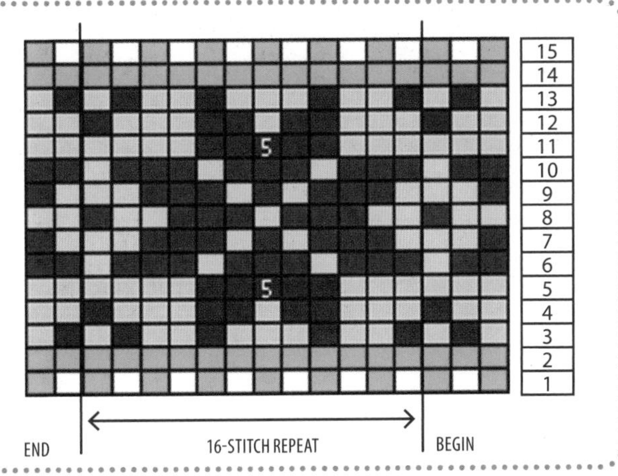

LISA'S DOUBLE STAR KNEE-HIGHS

LISA'S DOUBLE STAR KNEE-HIGHS CHART

LEG BORDER

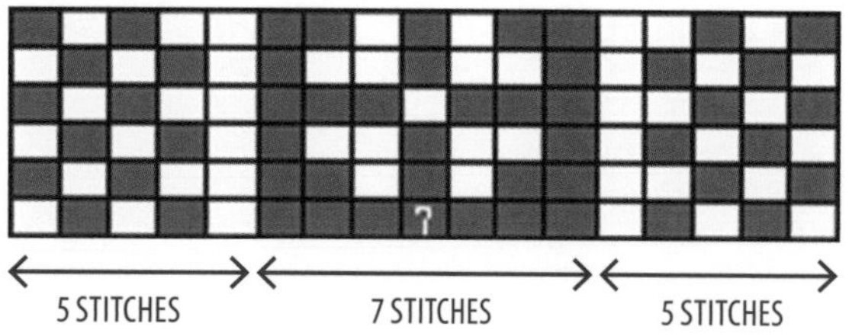

5 STITCHES 7 STITCHES 5 STITCHES

FOOT BORDER

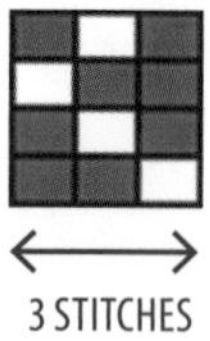

3 STITCHES

SOLE

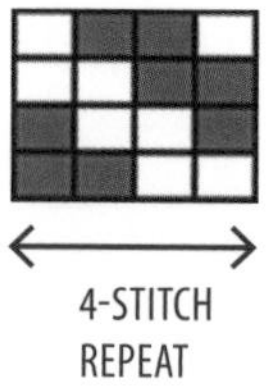

4-STITCH REPEAT

BLACK
FIG
CHARCOAL
CHESTNUT
LATTE
LINEN GREY
NATURAL
DARK YARN
LIGHT YARN

PATTERN

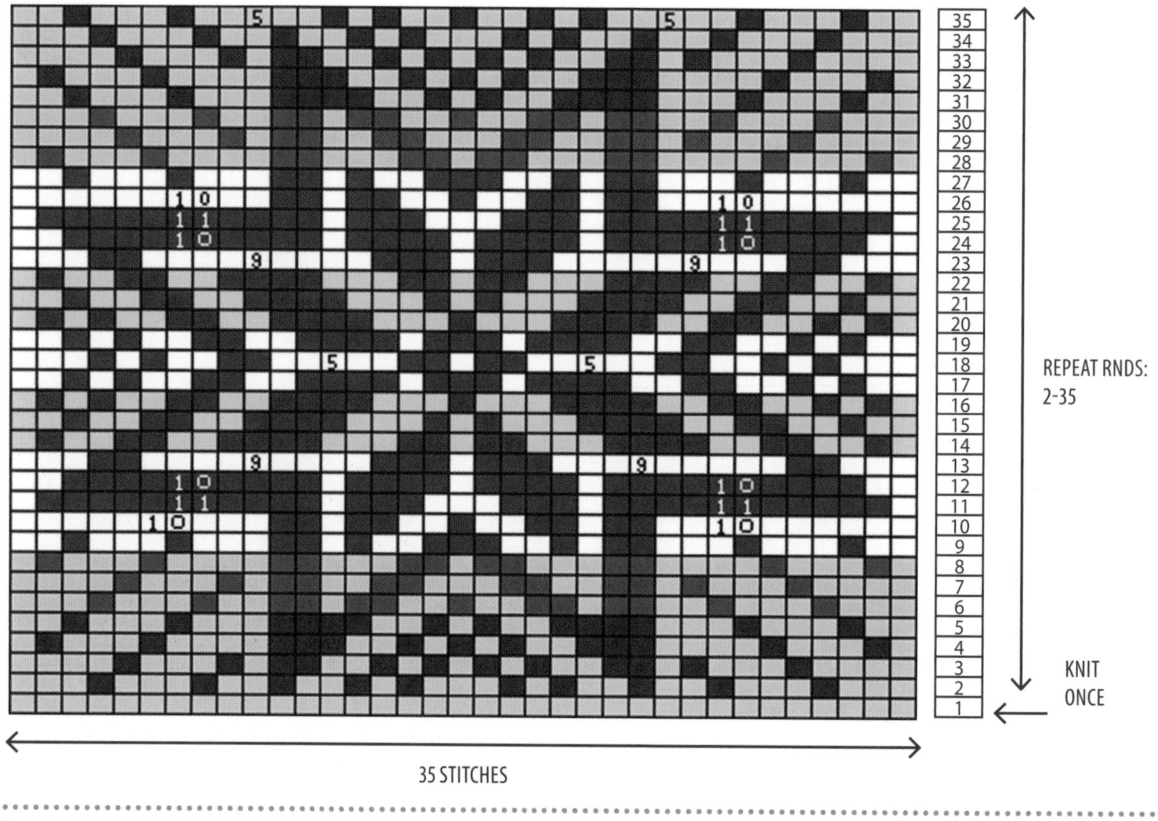

REPEAT RNDS: 2-35

KNIT ONCE

35 STITCHES

CREATE THE LOOK

Laurie's Chrysanthemum Mittens: **Page 48**

LAURIE'S CHRYSANTHEMUM KNEE-HIGHS

YARN

7 skeins of fingering weight yarn (approx 231yds [211m] per 1.76oz [50g]) in 6 different colors: 2 skeins of Natural and 1 skein each of Clematis, Curiosity, La Vie en Rose, Lilac (1) and Lilac (2)

The project shown was made using Madelinetosh Tosh Sock (100% merino wool, 4oz/114g, 395yds/361m) in Clematis and La Vie en Rose, Madelinetosh Tosh Merino Light (100% merino wool, 3.5oz/100g, 420yds/384m) in Curiosity, Valley Yarns Huntington (merino/nylon, 1.76oz/50g, 218yds/199m) in Natural, Sublime Baby Cashmere Merino Silk 4 Ply (merino/silk/cashmere, 1.76oz/50g, 186yds/170m) in Lilac (1) and Cascade Yarns Heritage 150 Solids (merino/nylon, 5.3oz/150g, 492yds/450m) in Lilac (2).

KNEE-HIGH CONSTRUCTION

Note: Unless otherwise indicated, Clematis is MC.

CUFF

With Clematis, cast on 96 sts. Work 20 rnds of the Corrugated Ribbing Pattern.

KNEE BORDER

Knit 2 rnds with Clematis, increasing 8 sts on first rnd—104 sts. Knit 13 rnds of the Sole Chart as follows: Knit 4 rnds with Curiosity/Lilac (2), knit Rnds 1–3, then Rnds 1–2 with Lilac (1)/Natural, knit 4 rnds with Curiosity/Lilac (2).

LEG

Knit 1 rnd with Clematis. Knit pattern Rnd 1 with Clematis only. Knit 3 repeats of Rnds 2–35 of the Pattern Chart while knitting the Leg Border and Knee-High Gusset Charts.

HEEL

Place 4 sts from each border on the same needle as the 35 Pattern Chart sts—43 sts. Knit the Heel Pattern in Curiosity (MC)/Natural (CC).

FOOT

Knit the Gusset Stripe Pattern beginning with Clematis (MC)/Lilac (2) (CC). Work Rnds 2–34 of the Pattern Chart coupled with the Foot Border Chart, Sole Chart and Gusset Stripe Pattern.

TOE BORDER

Knit 1 rnd with Clematis across Needle 1 while continuing the Sole Chart across Needles 2 and 3.

Knit the Toe Border Chart across Needle 1 while continuing the Sole Chart across Needles 2 and 3. Knit 1 rnd in Curiosity.

TOE

Knit the Toe with Curiosity (MC)/Natural (CC). Knit only 3 repeats of Toe decrease rnds before decreasing on every rnd.

CORRUGATED RIBBING PATTERN

Rounds 1-4: K2 Clematis p2 Lilac (2).

Rounds 5-6: K2 Curiosity, p2 Lilac (2).

Rounds 7-8: K2 La Vie en Rose, p2 Natural.

Rounds 9-12: K2 Lilac (1), p2 Natural.

Rounds 13-14: K2 La Vie en Rose, p2 Natural.

Rounds 15-16: K2 Curiosity, p2 Lilac (2).

Rounds 17-20: K2 Clematis p2 Lilac (2).

LAURIE'S CHRYSANTHEMUM KNEE-HIGHS CHART

TOE BORDER

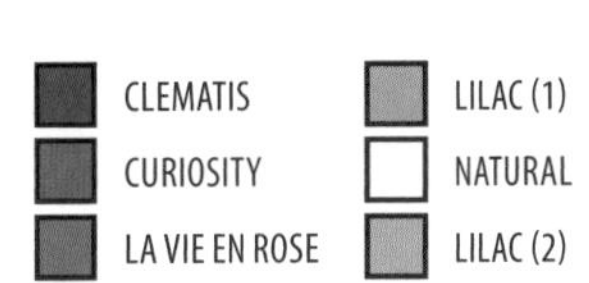

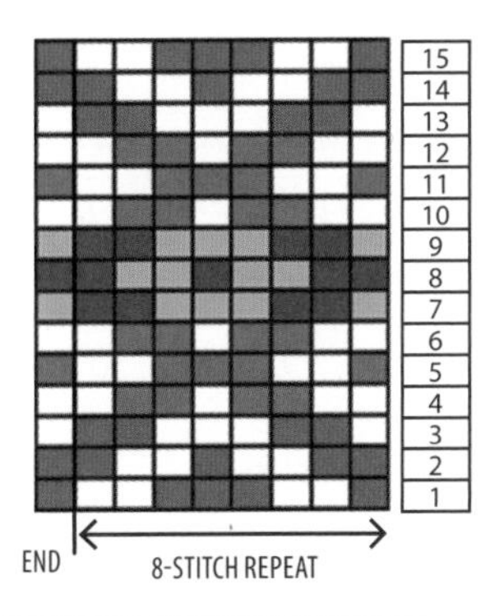

LAURIE'S CHRYSANTHEMUM KNEE-HIGHS

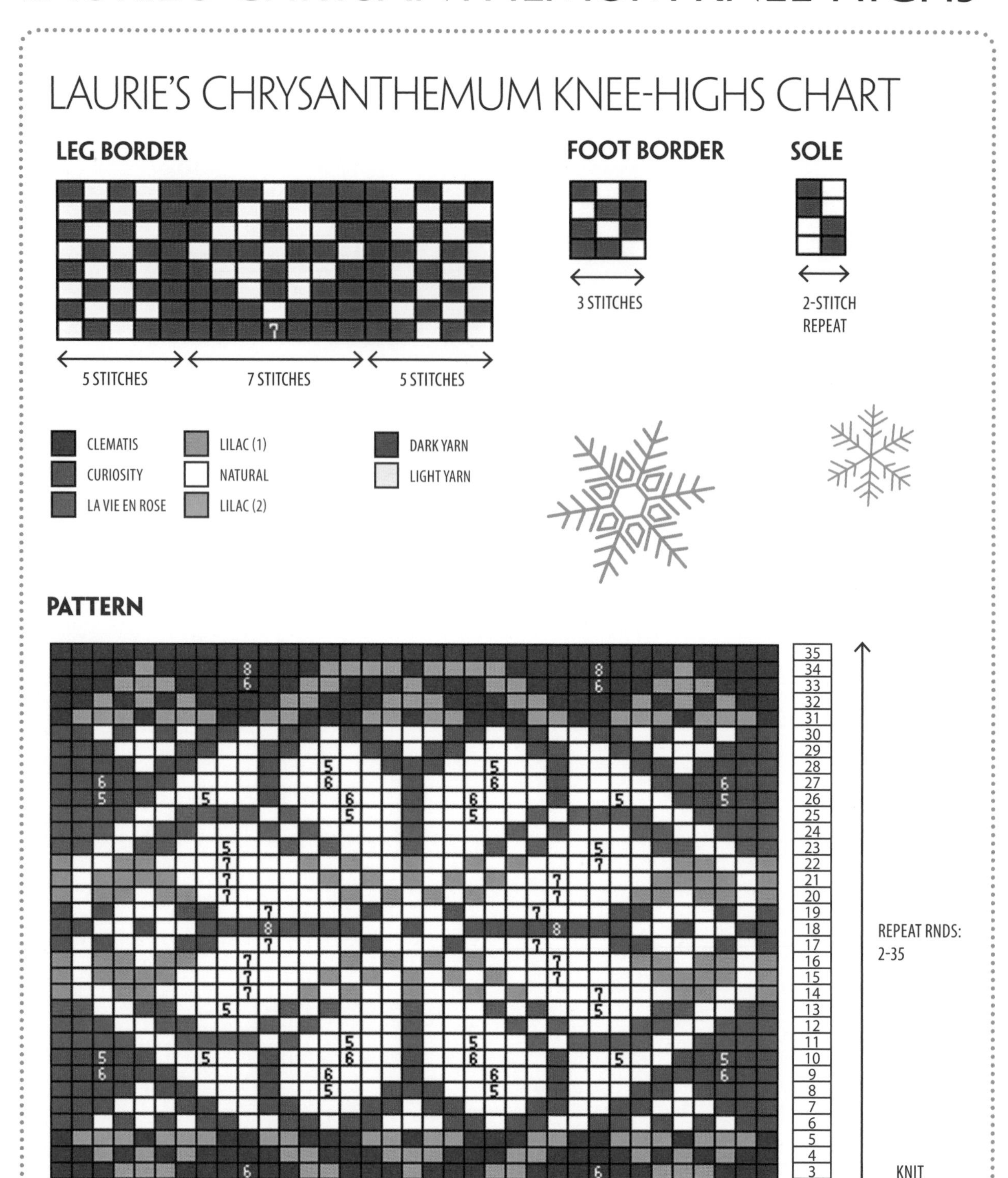

SABRINA'S OJO DE DIOS KNEE-HIGHS

YARN

6 skeins of fingering weight yarn (approx 231yds [211m] per 1.76oz [50g]) in 6 different colors: Black, Blue, Creme de Menthe, La Vie en Rose, Coral Rose and Pink

The project shown was made using Rio de la Plata Yarns Sock Solid (100% merino, 3.5oz/100g, 437yds/400m) in Coral Rose, Araucania Ranco Solid (wool/nylon, 3.5oz/100g, 376yds/344m) in Blue and Black, Araucania Itata Solid (wool/bamboo/silk, 3.5oz/100g, 430yds/393m) in Pink and Madelinetosh Tosh Sock (100% merino wool, 4oz/114g, 395yds/361m) in Creme de Menthe and La Vie en Rose.

KNEE-HIGH CONSTRUCTION

Note: Unless otherwise indicated, Black is MC.

CUFF

With Black, cast 96 sts onto 3 needles. Work 20 rnds of the Corrugated Ribbing Pattern.

KNEE BORDER

Knit 2 rnds with Black increasing 8 sts on the first rnd—104 sts. Knit 12 rnds of the Sole Chart as follows: Knit 4 rnds with Black/Coral Rose, knit 4 rnds with Black/Pink, knit 4 rnds with Black/Coral Rose. Knit 1 rnd with Black.

LEG

Work Rnd 1 with Black only. Knit Rnd 2 in the colors indicated by the pattern. Knit 3 repeats of Rnds 3–34 of the Pattern Chart with the Leg Border and Knee-High Gusset Charts.

HEEL

Place 5 sts from each border on the same needle as the 33 Pattern Chart sts—43 sts. Knit the first row of the Heel with Black. Knit the remaining Heel Pattern rows beginning with Row 2 with Black (MC)/La Vie en Rose (CC).

FOOT

Knit the Gusset Stripe Pattern beginning with Black (MC)/Blue (CC). Work Rnds 3–34 of the Pattern Chart coupled with the Foot Border Chart, Sole Chart and Gusset Stripe Pattern.

TOE BORDER

Knit 1 rnd in Black across Needle 1 while continuing the Sole Chart across Needles 2 and 3.

Knit the Toe Border Chart across Needle 1 while continuing the Sole Chart across Needles 2 and 3. Knit 1 rnd with Black.

TOE

Knit the Toe with Black (MC)/La Vie en Rose (CC).

CORRUGATED RIBBING PATTERN

Rnds 1–2: K2 Black, p2 Blue.

Rnds 3–4: K2 Black, p2 La Vie en Rose.

Rnds 5–6: K2 Black, p2 Creme de Menthe.

Rnds 7–8: K2 Black, p2 Coral Rose.

Rnds 9–12: K2 Black, p2 Pink.

Rnds 13–14: K2 Black, p2 Coral Rose.

Rnds 15–16: K2 Black, p2 Creme de Menthe.

Rnds 17–18: K2 Black, p2 La Vie en Rose.

Rnds 19–20: K2 Black, p2 Blue.

SABRINA'S OJO DE DIOS KNEE-HIGHS CHART

TOE BORDER

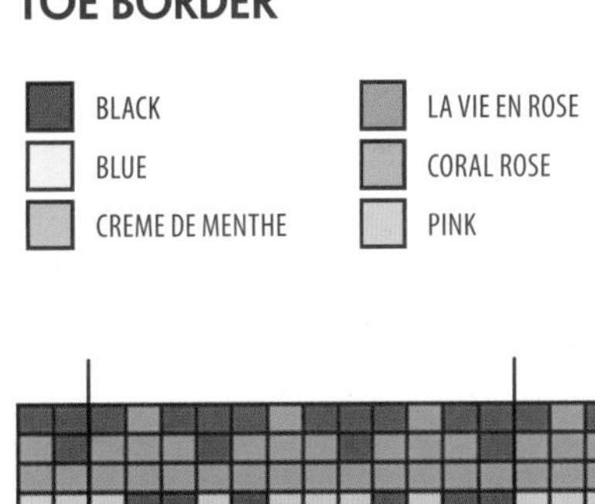

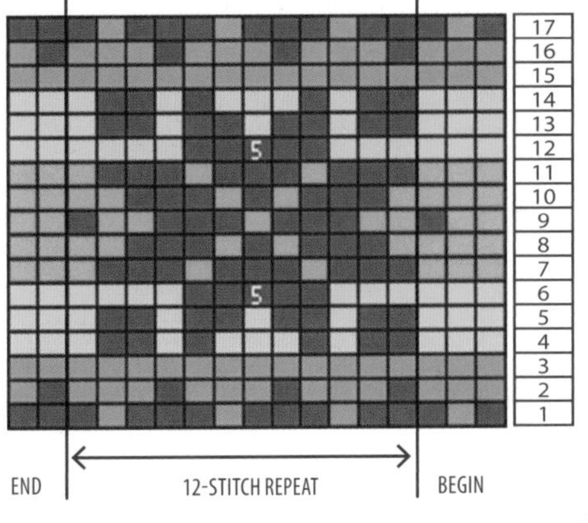

SABRINA'S OJO DE DIOS KNEE-HIGHS

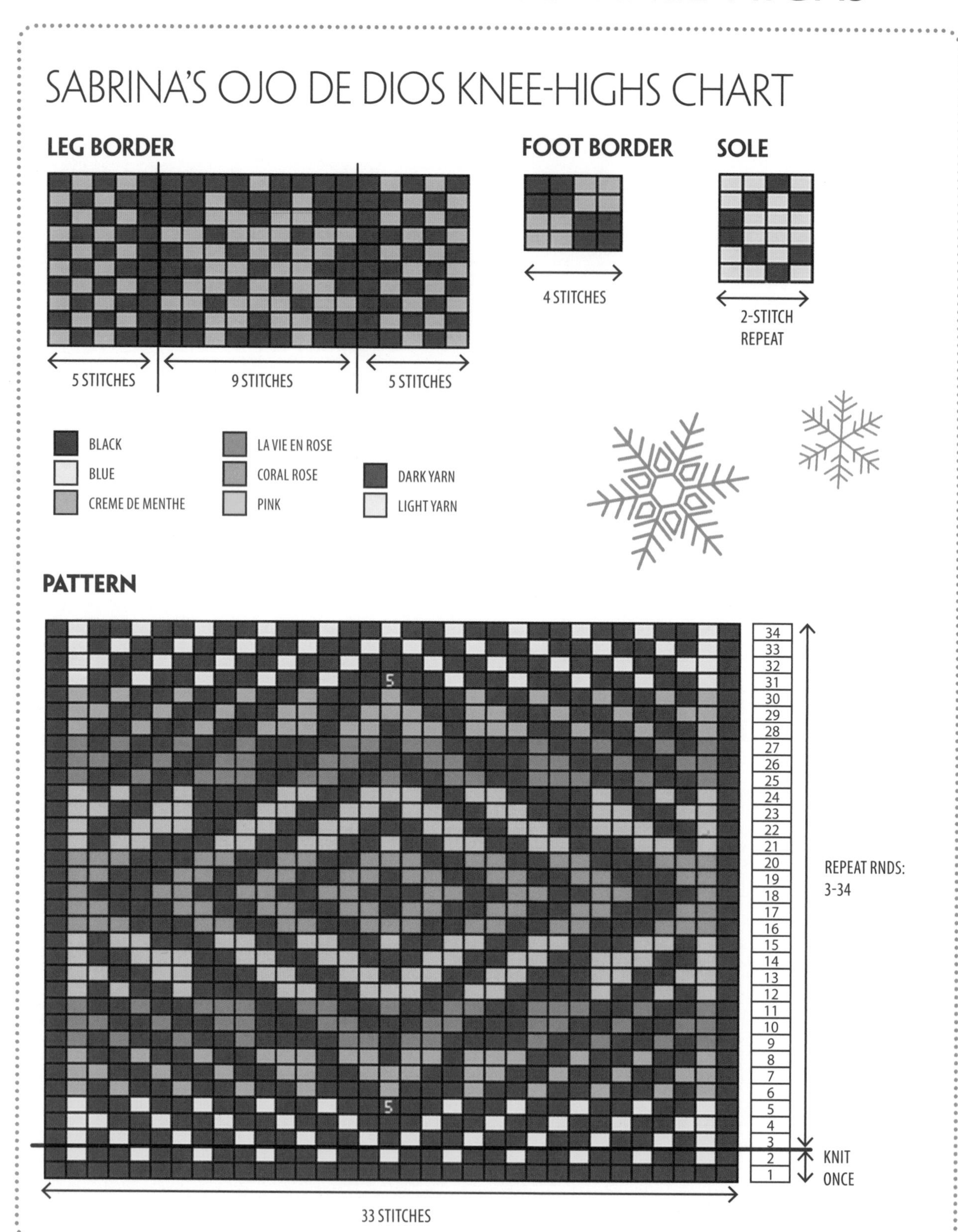

SABRINA'S OJO DE DIOS KNEE-HIGHS CHART
LEG BORDER
5 STITCHES
9 STITCHES
5 STITCHES
FOOT BORDER
4 STITCHES
SOLE
2-STITCH REPEAT
BLACK
BLUE
CREME DE MENTHE
LA VIE EN ROSE
CORAL ROSE
PINK
DARK YARN
LIGHT YARN
PATTERN
5
5
34
33
32
31
30
29
28
27
26
25
24
23
22
21
20
19
18
17
16
15
14
13
12
11
10
9
8
7
6
5
4
3
2
1
REPEAT RNDS: 3-34
KNIT ONCE
33 STITCHES

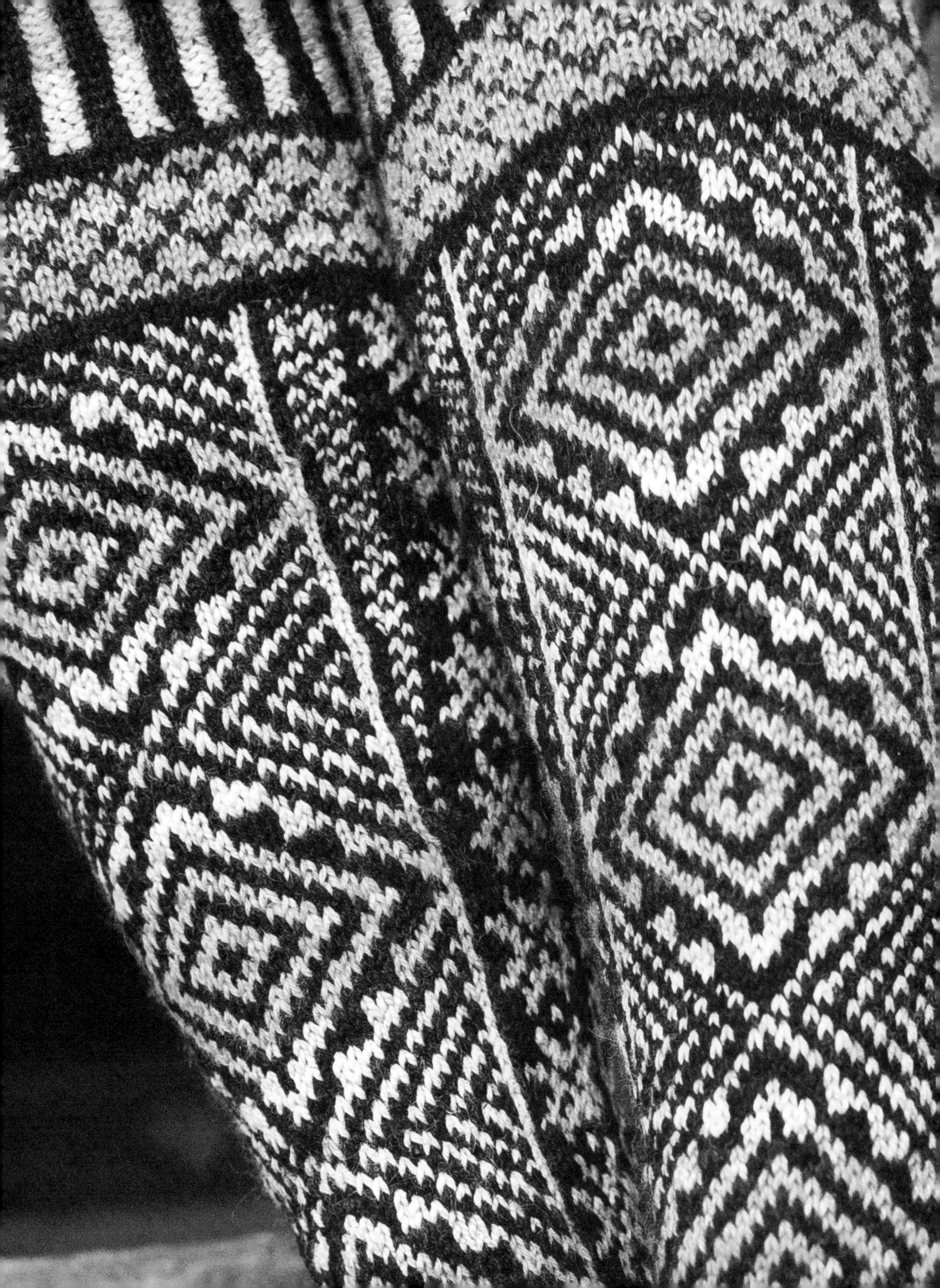

SABRINA'S OJO DE DIOS KNEE-HIGHS

ALTERNATE COLORWAY

YARN

6 skeins of fingering weight yarn (approx 231yds [211m] per 1.76oz [50g]) in 6 different colors: La Vie en Rose, Dahlia, Pink Panther, Lilac, Peach and Vanilla

The project shown was made using Madelinetosh Tosh Sock (100% merino wool, 4oz/114g, 395yds/361m) in La Vie en Rose, Madelinetosh Tosh Merino Light (100% merino wool, 3.5oz/100g, 420yds/384m) in Dahlia, Cherry Tree Hill/Louet Gems Fingering (100% merino wool, 1.76oz/50g, 185yds/169m) in Pink Panther, and Sublime Baby Cashmere Merino Silk 4-Ply (merino/silk/cashmere, 1.76oz/50g, 186yds/170m) in Lilac, Peach and Vanilla.

HEEL AND TOE

Knit the Heel and Toe with Dahlia (MC)/Pink Panther (CC).

CORRUGATED RIBBING PATTERN

Rnds 1–2: K2 Dahlia, p2 La Vie en Rose.

Rnds 3–4: K2 Dahlia, p2 Lilac.

Rnds 5–6: K2 Dahlia, p2 Pink Panther.

Rnds 7–8: K2 Dahlia, p2 Peach.

Rnds 9–12: K2 Dahlia, p2 Vanilla.

Rnds 13–14: K2 Dahlia, p2 Peach.

Rnds 15–16: K2 Dahlia, p2 Pink Panther.

Rnds 17–18: K2 Dahlia, p2 Lilac.

Rnds 19–20: K2 Dahlia, p2 La Vie en Rose.

KNEE-HIGH CONSTRUCTION

Note: Unless otherwise indicated, Black is MC.

CUFF

With Dahlia, cast 96 sts onto 3 needles. Work 20 rnds of the Corrugated Ribbing Pattern.

KNEE BORDER

Knit 2 rnds in Dahlia, increasing 8 sts on the first rnd—104 sts. Knit 12 rnds of the Sole Chart as follows: Knit 4 rnds with Dahlia/Vanilla, knit 4 rnds with Dahlia/Pink Panther, knit 4 rnds with Dahlia/Vanilla. Knit 2 rnds with Dahlia.

LEG

Work Rnd 1 with Dahlia only. Knit Rnd 2 in the colors indicated by the pattern. Knit 3 repeats of Rnds 3–34 of the Pattern Chart with the Leg Border and Knee-High Gusset Charts.

HEEL

Place 5 sts from each border on the same needle as the 33 Pattern Chart sts—43 sts. Knit the first row of the Heel with Dahlia. Knit the remaining Heel Pattern rows beginning with Row 2 with Dahlia (MC)/Pink Panther (CC).

FOOT

Knit the Gusset Stripe Pattern beginning with Dahlia (MC)/Vanilla (CC). Work Rnds 3–34 of the Pattern Chart coupled with the Foot Border Chart, Sole Chart and Gusset Stripe Pattern.

TOE BORDER

Knit 1 rnd in Dahlia across Needle 1 while continuing the Sole Chart across Needles 2 and 3.

Knit the Toe Border Chart across Needle 1 while continuing the Sole Chart across Needles 2 and 3. Knit 1 rnd with Dahlia.

TOE

Knit the Toe with Dahlia (MC)/Pink Panther (CC),

SABRINA'S OJO DE DIOS SOCKS CHART

ALTERNATE COLORWAY

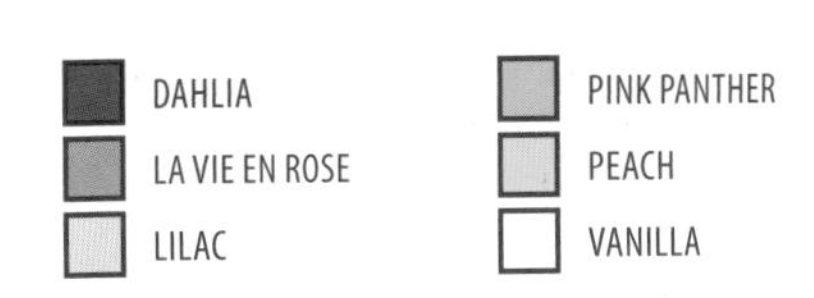

TOE BORDER

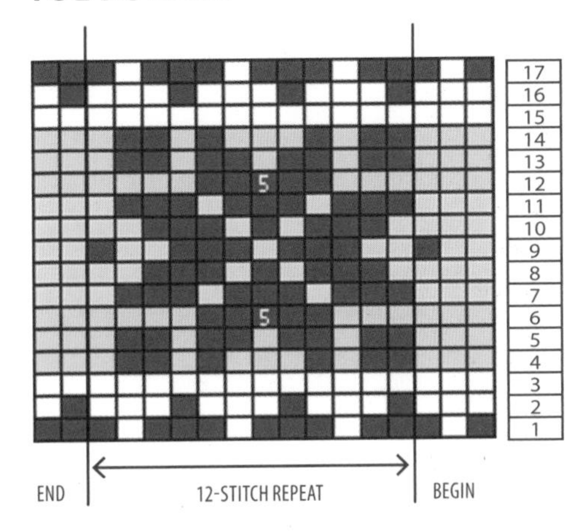

PATTERN

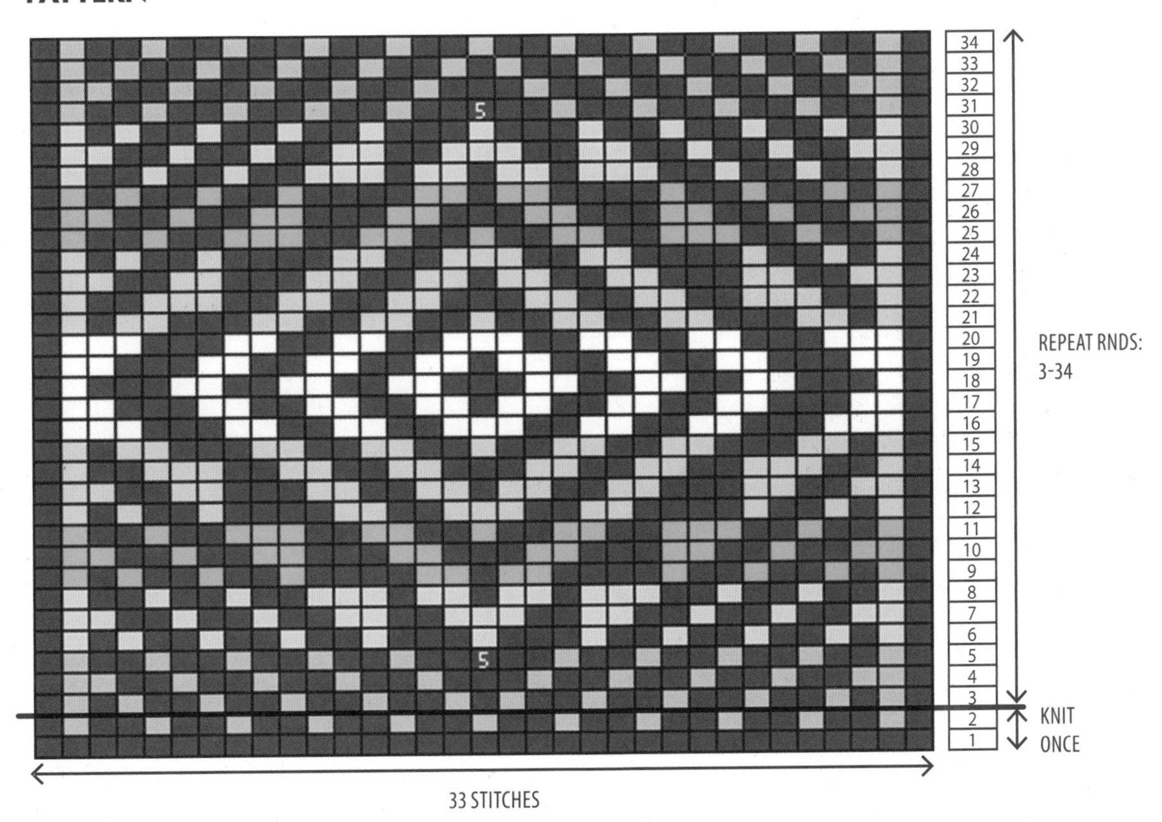

SUSAN'S STORM KNEE-HIGHS

YARN

6 skeins of fingering weight yarn (approx 231yds [211m] per 1.76oz [50g]) in 6 different colors: Bark, Latte, Baby Pink, Orange Sorbet, Blue and Baby Green

The project shown was made using Cascade Yarns Heritage 150 Solids (merino/nylon, 5.3oz/150g, 492yds/450m) in Bark and Araucania Itata Solid (wool/bamboo/silk, 3.5oz/100g, 430yds/393m) in Latte, Baby Pink, Orange Sorbet, Blue and Baby Green.

CORRUGATED RIBBING PATTERN

Rnds 1–4: K2 Bark, p2 Blue.

Rnds 5–6: K2 Bark, p2 Baby Green.

Rnds 7–8: K2 Bark, p2 Orange Sorbet.

Rnds 9–12: K2 Bark, p2 Latte.

Rnds 13–14: K2 Bark, p2 Orange Sorbet.

Rnds 15–16: K2 Bark, p2 Baby Green.

Rnds 17–20: K2 Bark, p2 Blue.

KNEE-HIGH CONSTRUCTION

Note: Unless otherwise indicated Bark is MC.

CUFF

With Bark, cast on 96 sts. Work 20 rnds of the Corrugated Ribbing Pattern.

KNEE BORDER

Knit 2 rnds with Bark, increasing 6 sts on first rnd—102 sts. Knit 12 rnds of the Sole Chart as follows: Knit 4 rnds with Bark/Blue, knit 5 rnds with Bark/Baby Green, knit 4 rnds with Bark/Blue. Knit 2 rnds with Bark while increasing 2 sts—104 sts.

LEG

Knit pattern Rnd 1 with Latte only. Knit 3 repeats of Rnds 2–35 of the Pattern Chart while knitting the Leg Border and Knee-High Gusset Charts.

HEEL

Place 3 sts from each border on the same needle as the 37 Pattern Chart sts—43 sts. Knit the Heel Pattern in Bark (MC)/Orange Sorbet (CC).

Knit the Gusset Stripe Pattern beginning with Bark (MC)/Latte (CC). Work Rnds 2–34 of the Pattern Chart coupled with the Foot Border Chart, Sole Chart and Gusset Stripe Pattern.

TOE BORDER

Knit 1 rnd with Orange Sorbet across Needle 1 while continuing the Sole Chart across Needles 2 and 3. Knit the Toe Border Chart across Needle 1 while continuing the Sole Chart across Needles 2 and 3. Knit 1 rnd with Orange Sorbet.

TOE

Knit the Toe with Bark (MC)/Orange Sorbet (CC). Knit only 3 repeats of Toe decrease rnds before decreasing on every rnd.

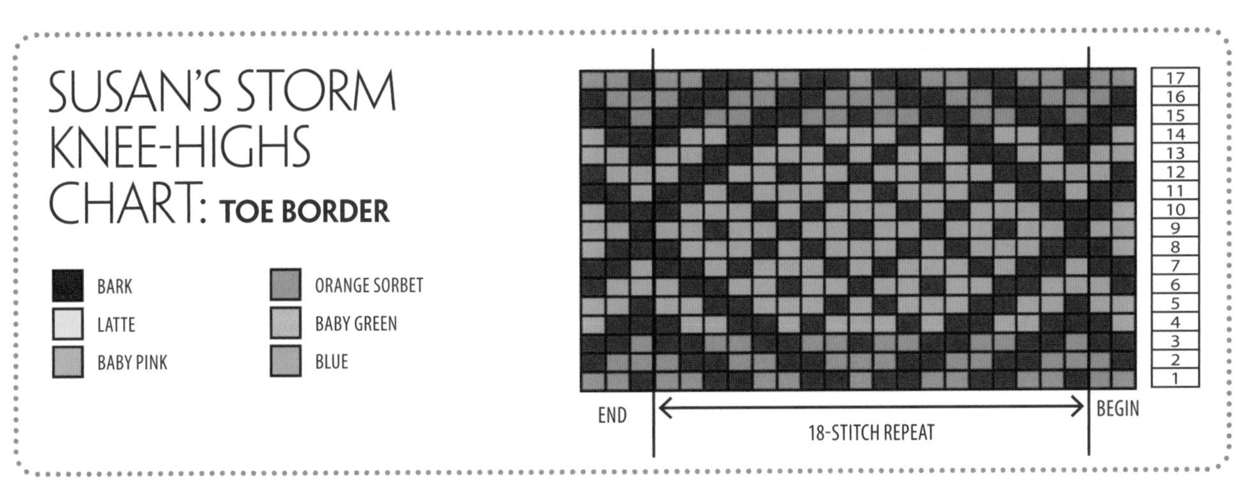

SUSAN'S STORM KNEE-HIGHS

SUSAN'S STORM KNEE-HIGHS CHART

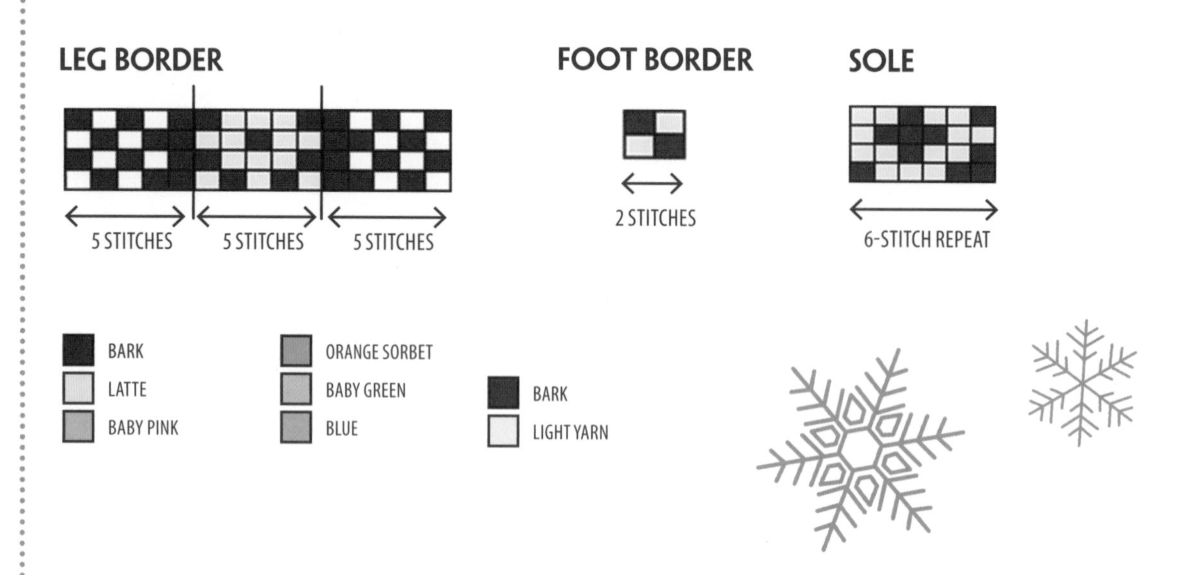

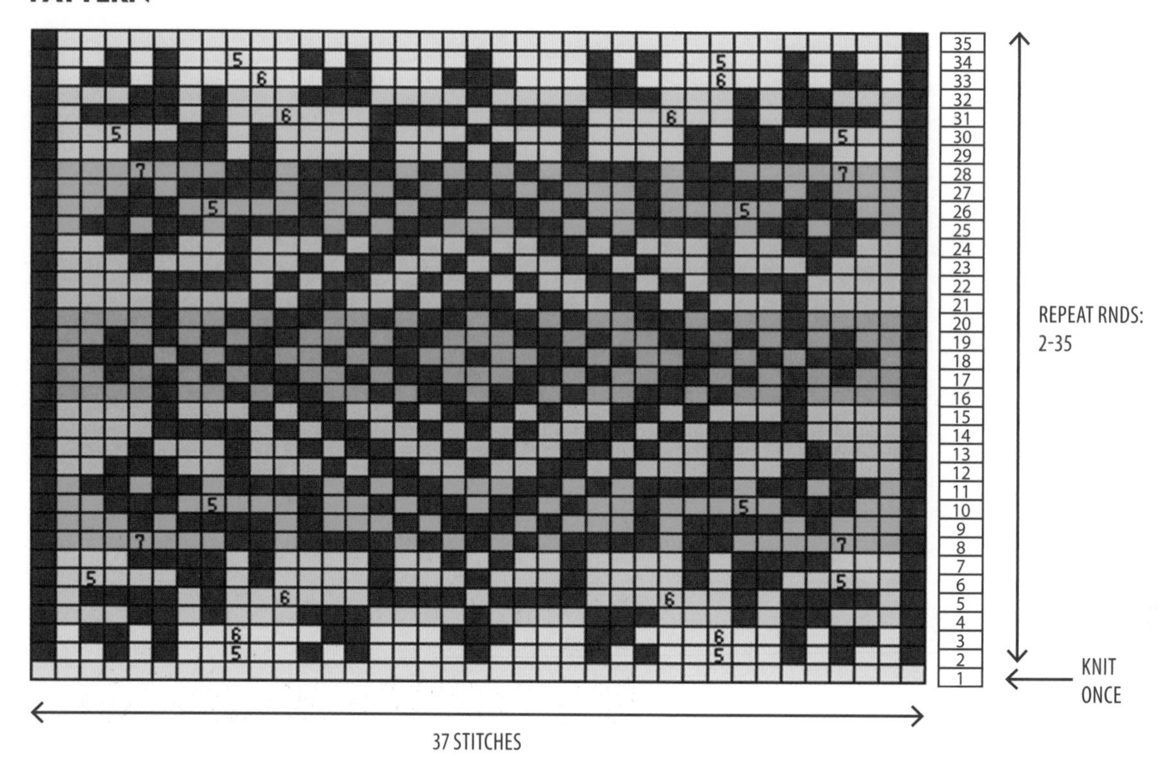

LEG WARMERS

SIZE

One size fits most women

MEASUREMENTS

Calf Circumference: 14" (35.5cm)

Leg Length: 15 1/2" (39.5cm)

Ankle Circumference: 10" (25.5cm)

NEEDLES

One 10" (25.5cm) set of US 3 (3.25mm) double-pointed needles or two 24" (61cm) circular needles

If necessary, change needle size to obtain correct gauge.

NOTIONS

Stitch markers

Tapestry needle

GAUGE

4" (10cm) = 26 sts and 26 rnds in salt-and-pepper pattern

Last year my daughter received a request for a pair of knitted leg warmers. I hadn't knit or designed leg warmers at the time, so Jenny found a pattern for a pair of simple cable leg warmers. Instead of gussets, the pattern changed the needle size to reduce the calf to ankle circumference. I tried this technique while designing my first pair of knee-highs and it was a dismal failure. Therefore, when I designed the leg warmers featured in this book I knew that they would use side gussets. I also wanted leg warmers that were warm, sturdy and quick to knit. I chose a 50 percent wool/50 percent alpaca worsted-weight yarn, and I loved the results. These leg warmers are fun to knit; they're a good project for stranded knitting neophytes.

CUSTOMIZING THE LEG WARMERS

For shorter leg warmers, reduce the number of rounds of ribbing. For longer leg warmers, add rounds to the ribbing or knit the optional peerie pattern until the length is 2 1/2" (6cm) less than your desired length. Pick whichever colors please you.

For wider leg warmers, add a stitch to each side of the gusset. Each pair of stitches will add about 3/4" (2cm) to the circumference. For narrower leg warmers, remove a stitch from each side of the gusset. Do this by starting the gusset after the first stitch decrease.

You may also add elastic between the layers of ribbing to ensure that the leg warmers stay up.

JEANNE'S SUNBURST LEG WARMERS

YARN

7 skeins of worsted weight yarn (approx 215 yds [198m] per 3.5oz [100g]) in 6 different colors: 2 skeins of Lobster Mix and 1 skein each of Grove Mix, Melon Mix, Pastel Blue, Periwinkle Mix and Pastel Pink

The project shown was made using Berroco Ultra Alpaca (alpaca/wool, 3.5oz/100g, 215yds/198m) in Lobster Mix, Grove Mix, Melon Mix, Pastel Blue, Periwinkle Mix and Pastel Pink.

CORRUGATED RIBBING PATTERN

Rounds 1-3: K2 Lobster Mix, p2 Periwinkle Mix.

Rounds 4-6: K2 Lobster Mix, p2 Melon Mix.

Rounds 7-9: K2 Lobster Mix, p2 Grove Mix.

Rounds 10-12: K2 Lobster Mix, p2 Melon Mix.

Rounds 13-15: K2 Lobster Mix, p2 Periwinkle Mix.

LEG WARMERS

With Lobster Mix, cast on 80 sts.

SELVEDGE

Work 11 rnds of corrugated ribbing as follows: K2 Lobster Mix, p2 Periwinkle Mix.

Hem Rnd: Purl 1 rnd with Lobster Mix.

CALF RIBBING

Knit 15 rnds of the Corrugated Ribbing Pattern. Increase 4 sts on the last rnd—84 sts.

With Lobster Mix, k31, pm, k11, pm, k31, pm, k11.

LEG

Knit Rnds 1–2 of the Pattern Chart with the Gusset Chart. Knit 2 repeats of Rnds 3–36 of the Pattern Chart with the Gusset Chart.

Knit Each Rnd As: Knit the Pattern Chart, sm, knit the Gusset Chart, sm, knit the Pattern Chart, sm, knit the Gusset Chart.

Knit Gusset Decreases As: K2tog tbl, knit to last 2 sts, k2tog.

Knit Last Decrease Rnd As: Sl 1, k2tog, psso.

Knit 1 rnd with Lobster Mix.

Optional Border: Knit the optional border to increase the length until the length is 2½" (6.5cm) less than the desired length.

ANKLE RIBBING

Knit 15 rnds of the Corrugated Ribbing Pattern.

Hem Rnd: Purl 1 rnd with Lobster Mix.

SELVEDGE

Work 9 rnds of corrugated ribbing as follows: K2 Lobster Mix, p2 Periwinkle Mix.

Bind off with Lobster Mix.

FINISHING

Weave in all ends. Turn to inside. Fold selvedges at Hem Rnds and tack into place. Block.

JEANNE'S SUNBURST LEG WARMERS

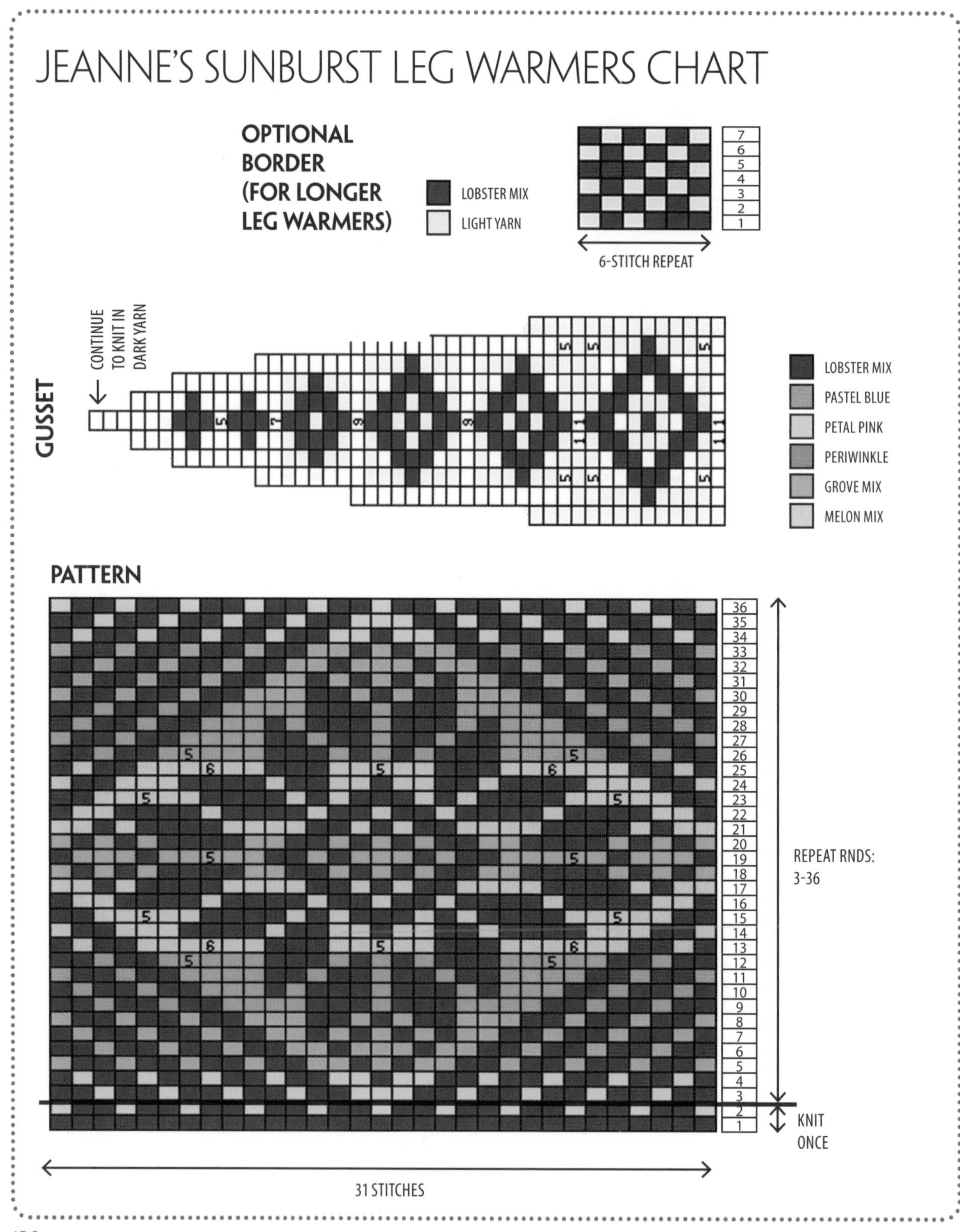

JENNY'S MAZE LEG WARMERS

YARN

6 skeins of worsted weight yarn (approx 215 yds [198m] per 3.5oz [100g]) in 6 different colors: Chianti, Admiral Mix, Candy Floss Mix, Light Gray, Boysenberry Mix and Couscous

The project shown was made using Berroco Ultra Alpaca (merino/nylon, 5.3oz/150g, 492yds/450m) in Chianti, Admiral Mix, Candy Floss Mix, Light Gray, Boysenberry Mix and Couscous.

CORRUGATED RIBBING PATTERN

Rnds 1–3: K2 Admiral Mix, p2 Light Gray.

Rnds 4–6: K2 Boysenberry Mix, p2 Candy Floss Mix.

Rnds 7–9: K2 Chianti, p2 Couscous.

Rnds 10–12: K2 Boysenberry Mix, p2 Candy Floss Mix.

Rnds 13–15: K2 Admiral Mix, p2 Light Gray.

LEG WARMERS

With Admiral Mix, cast on 80 sts.

SELVEDGE

Work 11 rnds of corrugated ribbing as follows: K2 Admiral Mix, p2 Light Gray.

Hem Rnd: Purl 1 rnd with Admiral Mix.

CALF RIBBING

Knit 15 rnds of the Corrugated Ribbing Pattern. Increase 4 sts on the last rnd—84 sts.

MAIN PATTERN

Knit Rnd 1 of the Pattern Chart with the Gusset Chart. Knit 2 repeats of Rnds 2–34 of the Pattern Chart with the Gusset Chart. Knit the first rnd with Admiral Mix only, placing markers as follows: K31, pm, k11, pm, k31, pm, k11—84 sts.

Knit Each Subsequent Rnd As: Knit the Pattern Chart, sm, knit the Gusset Chart, sm, knit the Pattern Chart, sm, knit the Gusset Chart.

Knit Gusset Decreases As: K2tog tbl, knit to last 2 sts, k2tog.

Knit Last Decrease Rnd As: Sl 1, k2tog, psso.

Continue to knit the 1 remaining gusset stitch using the dark yarn.

Knit 1 rnd with Admiral Mix.

Optional Border: Knit the Optional Border Chart to increase the length until the length is 2½" (6.5cm) less than the desired length.

ANKLE RIBBING

Work 15 rnds of the Corrugated Ribbing Pattern.

Hem Rnd: Purl 1 rnd with Admiral Mix.

SELVEDGE

Work 9 rnds of corrugated ribbing as follows: K2 Admiral Mix, p2 Light Gray.

Bind off with Admiral Mix.

FINISHING

Weave in all ends. Turn to inside. Fold Selvedges at Hem Rnds and tack into place. Block.

JENNY'S MAZE LEG WARMERS

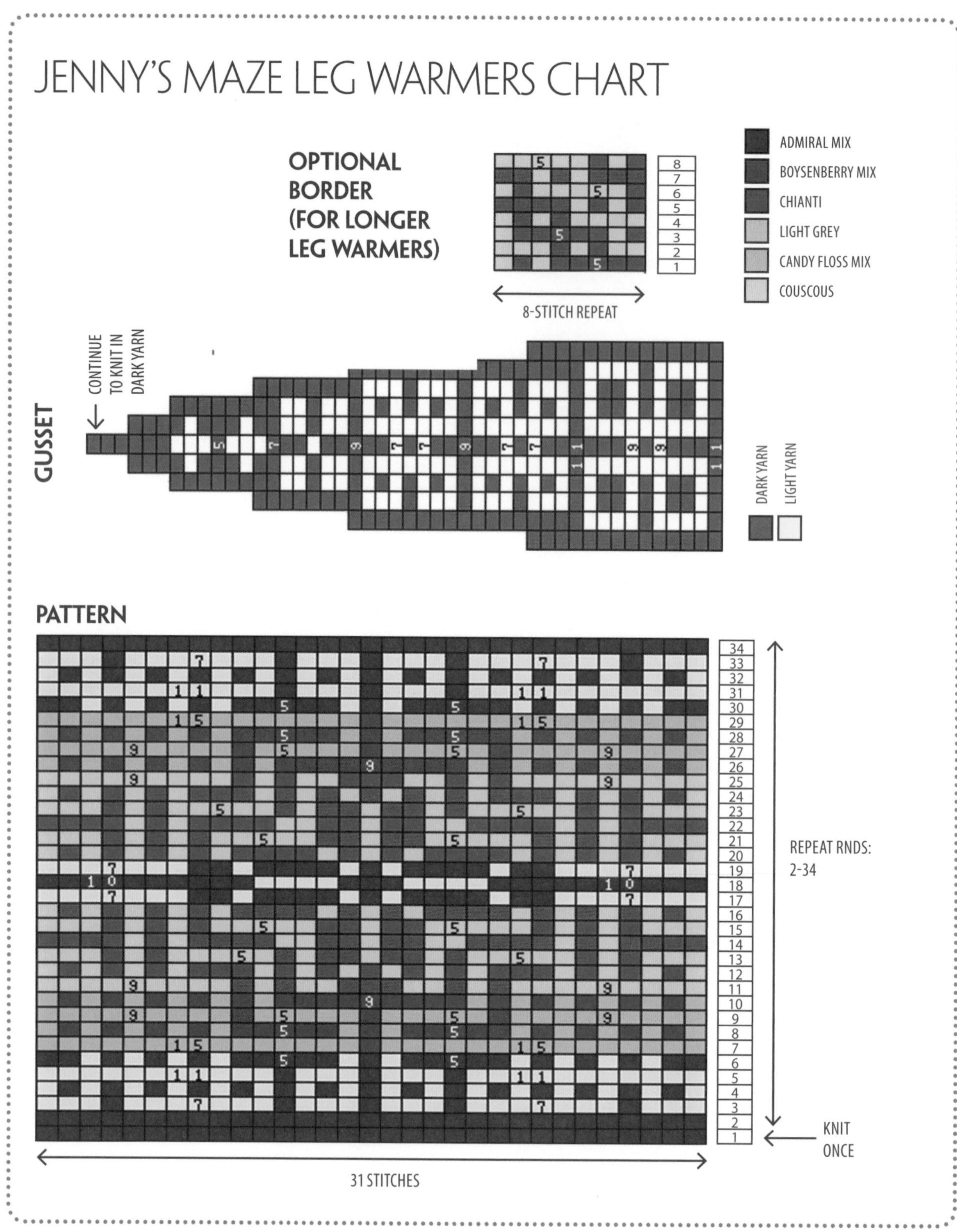

JENNY'S MAZE LEG WARMERS CHART
OPTIONAL BORDER (FOR LONGER LEG WARMERS)
8-STITCH REPEAT
ADMIRAL MIX
BOYSENBERRY MIX
CHIANTI
LIGHT GREY
CANDY FLOSS MIX
COUSCOUS
GUSSET
CONTINUE TO KNIT IN DARK YARN
DARK YARN
LIGHT YARN
PATTERN
REPEAT RNDS: 2-34
KNIT ONCE
31 STITCHES

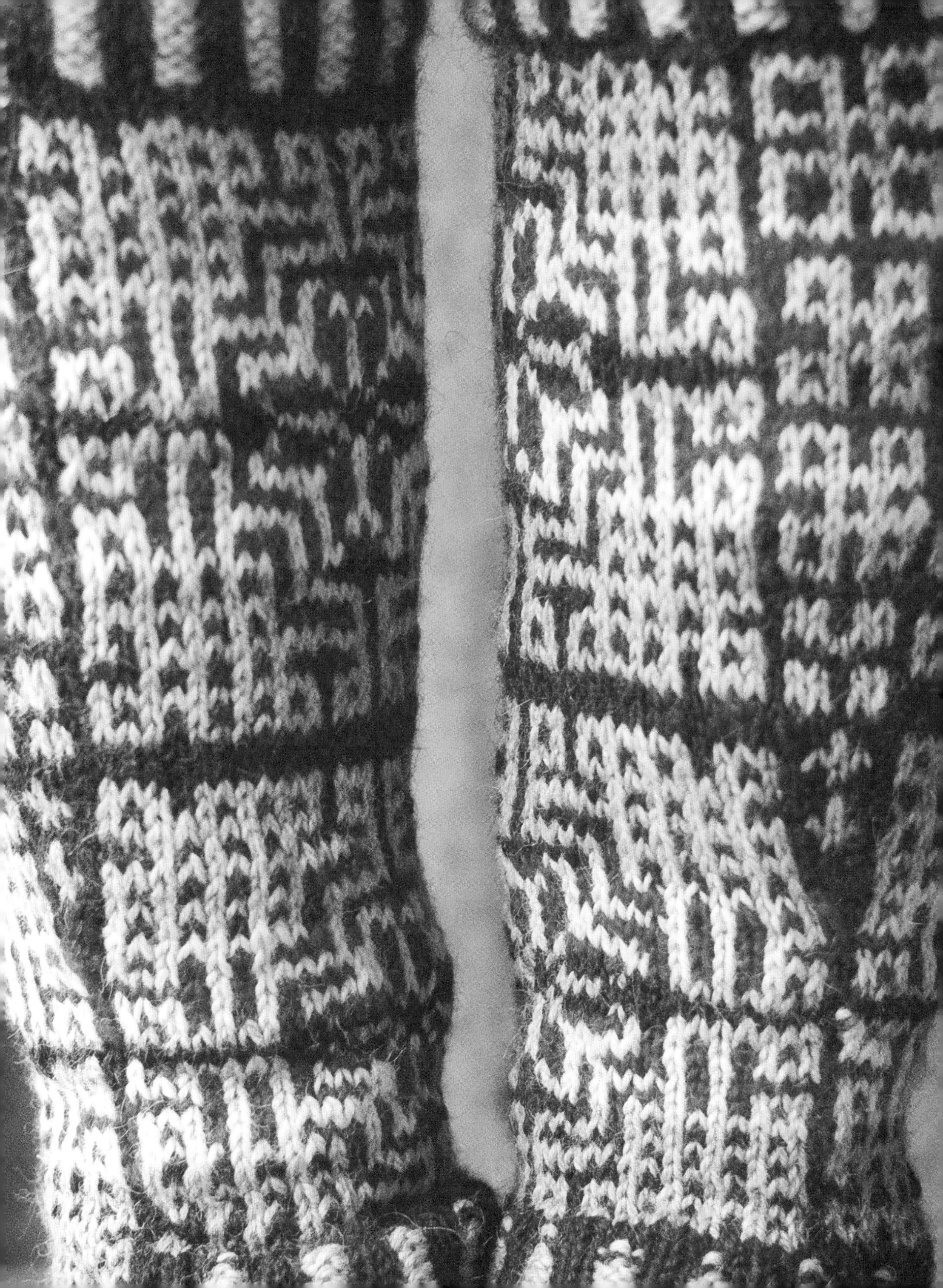

PATTY'S CELTIC CROSS LEG WARMERS

YARN

6 skeins of worsted weight yarn (approx 215 yds [198m] per 3.5oz [100g]) in 5 different colors: 2 skeins of Winter White and 1 skein each of Oceanic Mix, Turquoise Mix, Henna and Redwood Mix

The project shown uses one skein each Berroco Ultra Alpaca (merino/nylon, 5.3oz/150g, 492yds/450m) in Winter White, Oceanic Mix, Turquoise Mix, Henna and Redwood Mix.

CORRUGATED RIBBING PATTERN

Rnds 1–3: K2 Oceanic Mix, p2 Winter White.

Rnds 4–6: K2 Turquoise Mix, p2 Winter White.

Rnds 7–9: K2 Redwood Mix, p2 Winter White.

Rnds 10–12: K2 Turquoise Mix, p2 Winter White.

Rnds 13–15: K2 Oceanic Mix, p2 Winter White.

LEG WARMERS

With Oceanic Mix, cast on 80 sts.

SELVEDGE

Work 11 rnds of corrugated ribbing as follows: K2 Oceanic Mix, p2 Winter White.

Hem Rnd: Purl 1 rnd with Oceanic Mix.

CALF RIBBING

Knit 15 rnds of the Corrugated Ribbing Pattern. Increase 4 sts on the last rnd—84 sts.

MAIN PATTERN

With Oceanic Mix, k31, pm, k11, pm, k31, pm, k11.

Knit Rnds 1–2 of the Pattern Chart with the Gusset Chart. Knit 2 repeats of Rnds 3–34 of the Pattern Chart with the Gusset Chart.

Knit Each Rnd As: Knit the Pattern Chart, sm, knit the Gusset Chart, sm, knit the Pattern Chart, sm, knit the Gusset Chart.

Knit Gusset Decreases As: K2tog tbl, knit to last 2 sts, k2tog.

Knit Last Decrease Rnd As: Sl 1, k2tog, psso.

Knit 2 rnds with Oceanic Mix.

Optional Border: Knit the Optional Border Chart to increase the length until the length is 2½" (6.5cm) less than the desired length.

ANKLE RIBBING

Knit 15 rnds of the Corrugated Ribbing Pattern.

Hem Rnd: Purl 1 rnd in Oceanic Mix.

SELVEDGE

Work 9 rnds of corrugated ribbing as follows: K2 Oceanic Mix, p2 Winter White.

Bind off with Oceanic Mix.

FINISHING

Weave in all ends. Turn to inside. Fold Selvedges at Hem Rnds and tack into place. Block.

PATTY'S CELTIC CROSS LEG WARMERS

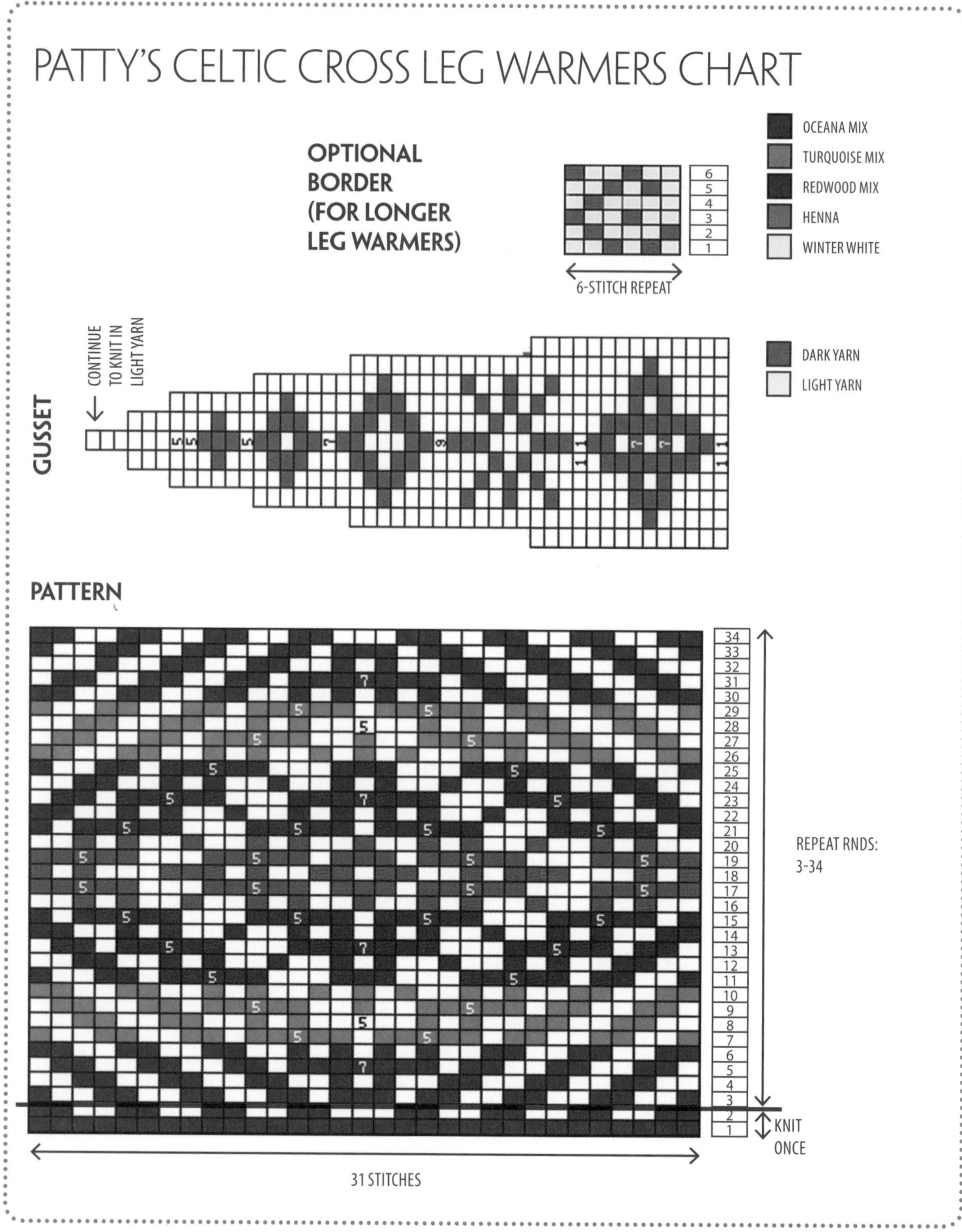

GENERAL KNITTING INFORMATION

ABBREVIATIONS

beg	begin(s)
dec	decrease
dpn(s)	double-pointed needles
foll	follow(s)
inc	increase
incL	left lifted increase
incR	right lifted increase
k	knit
k2tog	knit 2 together
m1	make 1
m1p	make 1 purl
p	purl
pm	place marker
psso	pass slipped stitch over
p2sso	pass 2 slipped stitches over
rem	remain(s)
rep	repeat
rnd(s)	round(s)
RS	right side
skp	slip, knit, pass slipped stitch over
sl	slip
ssk	slip, slip, knit
st(s)	stitch(es)
St st	Stockinette stitch
tbl	through back loop
tog	together
WS	wrong side
yo	yarn over

KNITTING NEEDLE SIZES

US	Metric
0	2mm
1	2.25mm
1½	2.5mm
2	2.75mm
2½	3mm
3	3.25mm
4	3.5mm
5	3.75mm
6	4mm
7	4.5mm
8	5mm
9	5.5mm
10	6mm
10½	6.5mm
	7mm
	7.5mm
11	8mm
13	9mm
15	10mm
17	12mm
19	16mm
35	19mm
36	20mm

CASTING ON

Turkish Cast On

All fingers, thumbs and mitten crowns begin with the Turkish cast on, which is typically used in toe-up socks.

Use two 6" (15cm) double-pointed needles. Wrap the yarn over the bottom needle. Wrap the yarn under then over the top needle. Wrap the yarn under then over the bottom needle.

Repeat this process until you have half of the required number of stitches on each needle. For example, if the directions indicate that you should cast on 6 stitches, cast 3 stitches on each needle.

Knit across the stitches on the top needle. Carefully reverse the needles so that the top needle is on the bottom.

Knit each of the stitches on the top needle through the back loops.

INCREASES

I use incR and incL lifted increases, but you can use m1 increases if you wish.

incL (left lifted increase): With your right needle, pick up the stitch one row below the stitch on the left needle. Knit this stitch.

incR (right lifted increase): With your right needle, pick up the stitch two rows below the stitch on the right needle. Knit this stitch.

m1 (make one): With your right needle, pick up the bar between the stitches on the left and right needles. Twist this stitch (to tighten it), and then knit it.

YARN WEIGHT GUIDELINES

Since the names given to different weights of yarn can vary widely depending on the country of origin or the yarn manufacturer's preference, the Craft Yarn Council of America has put together a standard yarn weight system to impose a bit of order on the sometimes unruly yarn labels. Look for a picture of a skein of yarn with a number 0–6 on most kinds of yarn to figure out its "official" weight. The information in the chart below is taken from www.yarnstandards.com.

	SUPER BULKY (6)	BULKY (5)	MEDIUM (4)	LIGHT (3)	FINE (2)	SUPERFINE (1)	LACE (0)
WEIGHT	SUPER-CHUNKY, BULKY, ROVING	CHUNKY, CRAFT, RUG	WORSTED, AFGHAN, ARAN	LIGHT WORSTED, DK	SPORT, BABY, 4PLY	SOCK, FINGERING, 2PLY, 3PLY	FINGERING, 10-COUNT CROCHET THREAD
KNIT GAUGE RANGE*	6–11 STS	12–15 STS	16–20 STS	21–24 STS	23–26 STS	27–32 STS	33–40 STS
RECOMMENDED NEEDLE RANGE**	11 (8MM) AND LARGER	9 TO 11 (5.5MM–8MM)	7 TO 9 (4.5MM–5.5MM)	5 TO 7 (3.75MM–4.5MM)	3 TO 5 (3.25MM–3.75MM)	1 TO 3 (2.25MM–3.25MM)	000 TO 1 (1.5MM–2.25MM)

Notes: * Gauge (tension) is measured over 4" (10cm) in Stockinette (stocking) stitch
** US needle sizes are given first, with UK equivalents in brackets

SUBSTITUTING YARNS

If you substitute yarn, be sure to select a yarn of the same weight as the yarn recommended for the project.

Even after checking that the recommended gauge on the yarn you plan to substitute is the same as for the yarn listed in the pattern, make sure to knit a swatch to ensure that the yarn and needles you are using will produce the correct gauge.

In the instructions for the projects, I have favored US knitting terms. Refer to this box for the UK equivalent.

US TERM	UK TERM
bind off	cast off
gauge	tension
stockinette stitch	stocking stitch

METRIC CONVERSION CHART

To convert	to	multiply by
Inches	Centimeters	2.54
Centimeters	Inches	0.4
Feet	Centimeters	30.5
Centimeters	Feet	0.03
Yards	Meters	0.9
Meters	Yards	1.1

INDEX

DEDICATION

To those whose lives have been touched by cancer.

ACKNOWLEDGMENTS

Many individuals helped make this book a reality, and I would like to thank them for their support and encouragement.

Thanks to my editor, Rachel Scheller, for guiding me through the production phases. Thank you to book designer, Anna Fazakerley, and to the photographers, Corrie Schaffeld and Al Parrish.

I'd also like to thank my husband, John, who tolerated the many bins of yarn filling the family room, and my daughter, Jenny, for test-knitting the tams.

I'd like to thank the doctors, nurses, staff and patients of Mid-Illinois Hematology and Oncology Associates. As in my previous book, I knit many of the items displayed in this book during chemotherapy and I received many words of encouragement during my weekly chemotherapy sessions. Nine of the patterns are named after the chemotherapy nurses at MIHOA to show my appreciation to their dedication and concern for their patients.

Finally, I would like to thank the volunteers and staff at the Community Cancer Center of Bloomington-Normal for providing a wonderful environment to undergo chemotherapy.

ABOUT THE AUTHOR

Susan Anderson-Freed learned to knit at the age of nine from her grandmother and has since passed along the craft to her daughter, Jenny.

She retired as a Professor of Computer Science at Illinois Wesleyan University in July 2010 after more than thirty years of teaching.

Susan employed her expertise in Web page and Web Graphic Design to write her first knitting book, *Colorwork Creations*. The designs in this book were inspired by the bird carvings of her late father, Don Anderson. The projects were chosen for exhibit at Northeastern Wisconsin Technical College as part of the Art Initiative Movement. She has given knitting workshops in Illinois, Wisconsin and Minnesota.

Published by Krause Publications, a division of F+W Media, Inc., 10151 Carver Road, Suite 200 Blue Ash, Ohio 45242. (800) 289-0963.

First Edition.

www.fwmedia.com

16 15 14 13 12 5 4 3 2 1

Distributed in Canada by Fraser Direct
100 Armstrong Avenue
Georgetown, ON, Canada L7G 5S4
Tel: (905) 877-4411

Distributed in the U.K. and Europe by F&W MEDIA INTERNATIONAL
Brunel House, Newton Abbot, Devon, TQ12 4PU, England
Tel: (+44) 1626 323200, Fax: (+44) 1626 323319
Email: enquiries@fwmedia.com

Distributed in Australia by Capricorn Link
P.O. Box 704, S. Windsor NSW, 2756 Australia
Tel: (02) 4577-3555

SRN: W8636
ISBN-13: 978-1-4402-3026-4

Editor: Rachel Scheller
Designer: Anna Fazakerley
Production Coordinator: Greg Nock
Photographers: Corrie Schaffeld and Al Parrish

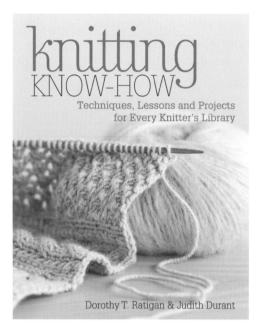